SOULS

A GENEALOGICAL COLLECTION

GWENDOLYN J HATCHER

Order this book online at www.trafford.com
or email orders@trafford.com

Most Trafford titles are also available at major online book retailers.

Printed in the United States of America.

ISBN: 978-1-4907-0899-7 (sc)
ISBN: 978-1-4907-0898-0 (hc)
ISBN: 978-1-4907-0897-3 (e)

Library of Congress Control Number: 2013914546

Trafford rev. 08/20/2013

 www.trafford.com

North America & international
toll-free: 1 888 232 4444 (USA & Canada)
fax: 812 355 4082

CONTENTS

Dedication vii

Introduction ix

Section One: New England Ancestry New Haven
   County, Connecticut and Massachusetts 1

Section Two: New York Ancestry 49

Section Three: Our Jackson Ancestors from
   New York and New Haven. 69

Section Four: Moving Toward the South;
   First Stop Philadelphia, then Delaware,
   Baltimore, and Washington DC 88

Section Five: Entering the South: Virginia 102

Section Six: North Carolina. 149

Section Seven: My Hometown and the Dubois
   Family Cheshire and Waterbury, CT. 175

Endnotes 199

In loving memory of my dad, the late Theodore W. Hatcher Jr., and my sister, the late Viola Dubois Hatcher, who rest in peace with the Lord. This publication is dedicated to all my ancestors and kin, particularly to my mother, Viola J. Hatcher; my sister Barbara J. Hatcher; my son, Watani Abdul Dubois Hatcher; and my aunt Natalie Douglas-Hardy, the former Natalie R. Hatcher.

Special thanks and recognition are given to all those who were and continue to be a major part of my life. I honor my ancestors and salute them for their courage.

I thank those who contributed to the gathering of information regarding my ancestors as follows: my mother, Viola J. Hatcher; my sister Dr. Barbara J. Hatcher; my aunt Natalie Douglas-Hardy; and my cousins Harold Garner, Asiila bintal Garner, Mary Jane Cherry (formerly Mary Jane Lewis), Dr. Dianne S. Hardison, Dr. Bruce Jackson, Katherine Jackson Harris, Leah Jackson, and last but not least, Margaret Moore. I enjoyed this journey.

Very special thanks to my husband for coping with me during this research of my ancestors. Bless you, Pastor.

"Remove not the ancient landmark, which thy fathers have set" (Proverbs 22:28) (KJV).

INTRODUCTION

After working for so long and being blessed with retirement, I have finally found time to research my ancestry. I have been at this for years, but suddenly, I felt this deep urge to complete this ancestral project. For some strange reason, I wanted to know all I could about my people who came before me. I knew some things, in fact, quite a few things, but I had a strong desire to know more. I wanted to know my complete blood lineage in spite of the fact that I knew from history that I would never know them all. In the earlier years, entire records were not kept on the African American as they mingled with the non-African people in the population, and they actually created babies together, some who are my ancestors. But except for one case, the French Dubois, I do not know with whom they mixed. This dilemma is quite common. You should expect the same if you decide to do your own family research.

In spite of it all, I started documenting and confirming my progenitors who I knew personally since I was a little child. I started first with my immediate family, and I began to build my family tree from the different branches, starting with my paternal side. It was quite interesting. I also began to contact my elders who knew others in our family tree that I had never met, and they shared stories with me about people and incidents that proved important in this genealogical research.

The more serious I got in this research, the more I began to feel the spirit connecting me to new things, including connecting me to others in search of their distant past. I found it rather astounding at first and even more amazing that I was not the only one interested in my ancestors, and I was not the only one who was beginning to uncover the facts about my existence. In fact, wherever I go now, I overhear or I actually converse with people talking about finding their roots and how much they have uncovered about their family's past. Others have had little or no success, and others just don't have the desire to know these things. You have to really want to know to participate in such a genealogical study. Nevertheless, there seems to be so much energy and excitement for those who are truly interested. I can attest to this. It's quite interesting and full of surprises.

Special recognition is given to Ancestry.com, the Church of Jesus Christ of Latter-day Saints and the National Archives and Records Administration for their efforts toward preserving and sharing US census and other ancestral records. I also thank the Commonwealth of Virginia for its extensive research of my ancestors and the historical designation of places my ancestors founded. I thank the city of Waterbury and the towns of Cheshire and Watertown and the Fairfax Board of Superiors and their staff for their contributions and the sharing of archived records. I do believe that God is in the midst of this mission at this very moment in time. For some strange reason, I really needed to know about myself.

I already knew quite a bit about my ancestors and the places from where many of them were originally born and raised because of the frequent conversations that occurred as we sat in our grandparents' homes or gathered for family reunions. Some of our ancestors had community status that was frequently acknowledged. Some were at the forefront of change.

At this particular point in time, I recognized that so many of my elders were passing, and I only had a few remaining who were in their nineties. Longevity has been a blessing to our family. Nevertheless, the fact that there are so few of my elders still living served as a clue that I had to quickly conduct interviews to gather as much as I could. We as a people are known for our oral traditions.

The skills that I developed over the years beginning with my studies at Howard University in Washington DC where I earned a bachelor degree in sociology helped to expedite this even further. To top it off, and fortunately for me, I had recently earned the distinguished title of retiree after serving for more than thirty-four years as a public servant. From the start of my professional training via a traditional black college until now, my interests remained strong in the social, cultural, and religious aspects of life. This carried over to my studies that led to my master of art in teaching from Trinity College, also in Washington DC, in which my field of study was art. I tried desperately to conduct genealogical research while working, but trying to fit productive time into my already busy schedule as a top official in county government was difficult. Not nearly enough progress had been made. I definitely know more now than when I started.

I would be remiss if I didn't take a moment to thank the educators in the various universities and colleges who conducted extensive research on the African American and on slavery both in the North and the South. Based on the fact that I was born and raised in the North and a great majority of my family were born, raised, or settled in the North as well, most of the research required was in the northeastern part of this country and particularly Connecticut, New York, and Massachusetts. Because of my strong and very long roots in New Haven, Connecticut, and other cities in New Haven County, quite a bit of information needed to tell my family's story came from Yale-New Haven Teachers Institute. I respect the work of all teachers, and I give them high recognition.

But my ancestry does not stop in the places listed above. In order to explore the lives and times of my complete ancient ancestry, a number of other places proved equally important from Philadelphia, Pennsylvania, to Baltimore, Maryland, to Washington DC, then Fairfax County, Virginia, and finally to North Carolina. The last two areas are where my southern roots began simultaneously with the beginning of my northern roots in Connecticut and New York.

"Remove not the ancient landmark, which thy fathers have set" (Proverbs 22:28). This is my favorite verse as it relates to this ancestral journey.

I can tell you that you need time to research your ancestry, and once you start, it becomes quite addicting as you work steadily to gain information and to locate and analyze reams of documents. Even though I knew of my Dubois heritage and the Odrick, Hatcher, Frisby, Jackson and Moore and other connections, I learned so much more through this ancestral search. In fact, I was surprised and honored to find so many of my ancestors listed on Ancestry.com as far back as the census of 1850 as well as discovering amazing facts about slavery in the North.

I was not told about slavery in the North by my elders nor did I learn about it in the schools. My elders who shared information with me may not have known themselves, and it is possible that the study of slavery in our educational institutions just did not make that distinction. I do know the focus was forever on the South where slavery endured for a longtime as part of the South's labor system and for the sole purpose of advancing the southern economy and the wealth of a few.

I must say that recent movies and literature on the topic of slavery in the South helped me grasp the true meaning of slavery as it existed in this land and other places. I found this institution hurtful and piercing to my heart, and the Southern renditions of slavery in the media, to include the movies, literally made me sick. So I avoided such topics as much as possible and instead stayed focused on the present and on our numerous accomplishments as a people. However, my curiosity began to peak as I started my own journey in search of my people.

I recently discovered that I am not the only one who is or was unaware of the fact that slavery existed in the North and that the black laws of the North applied to African Americans, free or not. I simply recall the North as a place where freedom existed for all no matter what one's ethnicity or race. "Give me your tired, your poor, your huddled masses yearning to breathe free." However, I discovered that the African American was fighting an uphill battle in the northern states and their movements as free people were very limited and restricted by the black laws in the earlier days. I thought I may have missed something in my studies until I recently discovered otherwise.

In a document entitled "Slavery in the North," Douglas Harper states that he kept running into people, most of them born and raised in "free" states, who had no idea there ever were slaves in the North. In addition, he discovered nothing in his search that indicated that blacks had been held in bondage in all thirteen of the original states.[1] I too was guilty of this lack of knowledge about the earlier days in the North until recently. Being born from generations of free people of color, I was under one big misconception as I am sure many are or have been. I was actually surprised at what I found.

But I was not surprised to find my ancestors from the North and from the South listed as mulatto. My heritage was obviously mixed. Being listed so early in the census was a clear indication that my ancestors were both freed people as well as free people of color. Since my family and I are New Englanders and New Yorkers from generations back, we were always told that our connection to slavery was probably nil, and I believe this probably holds true in most but not all instances. In spite of this, a new revelation did in fact occur as I discovered that slavery did exist in the North though the existence of this institution was much shorter and, at times, minimal when compared to what was endured by those in the South. During this search, I have found that this shorter time may have even included a few of my ancestors in bondage from the South. Many were freed years before the passing of the Emancipation Proclamation of 1865, while others were not.

I also cannot overlook the fact that there continue to be unknown ancestors who were obviously European who may have been born free or some may have been indentured servants. Having been in this country for three or possibly more than four hundred years, Indian ancestry could have been somewhere in the mix as well. I have found no hard evidence to support this, and it would have been so long ago. Just remember Indians and other Europeans were indentured servants or former slaves at some point in this ancestral history. African Americans were not the only ones who served in these capacities though the world would like us to think so.

In essence, many of my ancestors were free at some point in time and others for a very long time or forever. I do know that several of my ancestors on my father's side were listed as mulatto, and so was my mother's grandfather. European ancestry was for sure and the European ancestors may or may not have been exempt from slavery or servitude. The truth about most of their identities and ethnicities more than likely will never be known and will remain obscure and known only to those in the distant past.

But I know specifically of one ancestor who was a white master of French descent and who fathered two children by his Bahamian slave mistress. This mistress died in the Bahamas, and her name remains unknown. She would have been my fourth great-grandmother. My fourth great-grandfather Dr. James Dubois, a white French physician, brought two of his mixed children from the Bahamas to the United States, specifically Cheshire, Connecticut, where they were placed in gentleman's school. This fact is easily located in a plethora of documents regarding W. E. B. Du Bois and the DuBois genealogy. Fourth great-grandfather, James, must have dearly loved his mistress who supposedly passed before his journey back to the States, and he must have loved his sons to take on the challenge that he did. Unfortunately, he died and left no will for his children.[2]

Thumbing through the numerous documents written about and by W. E. B. Du Bois, it is common knowledge that the original Dubois members were Huguenots. They took possession of fourth great-grandfather's wealth and made it plain and clear that his sons, my third great-grandfather Alexander Dubois and his brother, my third great-granduncle John, were of color and were of a lesser status than the rest. It is suspected that John may have moved to New York and passed as white while third great-grandfather Alexander didn't pass though he was very light in complexion.

Years ago, my father told me about cousins who lived in New York who did not relate to their African American family for fear of losing their white identity. He had never met them. They were probably the children born to my third great-granduncle John and their offspring. I would expect within time some may have appeared slightly tan in color revealing their Bahamian ancestry. Genes have a way of showing up years later. I found a number of African American Dubois members from New York who were listed as mulatto at one time. I have not yet researched or made any family connections but it is a strong possibility that they were descendants of great-granduncle John.

Free People of Color

We were told by our Northern ancestors that we were "free people of color," and we needed to be proud of this. We needed to honor this unique and rewarding phenomenon. Yet in spite of our numerous family gatherings, not many of our family discussions ever centered on the struggles felt by our ancient ancestors abroad or even in the North, particularly as New Yorkers and New Englanders. Come to think about it, our conversations did not include the struggles at all. Instead, our elders discussed the makeup of our families, some of the family member's accomplishments and important family-related events, and more importantly their expectations of us: be good and law-abiding citizens.

I now know that being free people of color did not exempt our progenitors from extremely trying and extremely frustrating times. Yet in the midst of it all, some of my ancestors were actually leaders in paving the way toward freedom, equality, and respect for our people. Even so, my more recent ancestors were basically silent about these trying affairs. They may not have known themselves since some of these matters occurred long before even their time. Also, research was not as readily available as it is today. In spite of it all, for us, the focus was to always look forward and to achieve whatever we could and to demand respect and to give it back to those who deserve it. My family is filled with firsts, and my people have been basically go-getters throughout our ancestry. I will discuss some of those firsts from time to time in this writing.

But what I have learned is that in spite of freedom, my progenitors were subjected to discrimination and racism. This has not been totally eradicated even today. Though some climbed past the remnants of slavery and serfdom, and though so many of my ancestors were listed as mulatto as far back as the 1850s when free African Americans were enumerated with their names and other pertinent information, we were still considered less than those who were full-blooded white, or at least they thought they were. Sometimes they knew they weren't and passed as such in spite of their personal knowledge. They considered this a blessing, and it allowed them to share the same rights, pleasures, and schooling as their white counterparts.

Prior to 1850, slaves were listed only as a number with no unique identifiers other than the name of the master by whom they were held in most cases. Occasionally, they may have had at least a nickname. Any person had to be a free inhabitant to be listed by his or her full name in the 1850 census. Important is the fact that so many people had the same name as others just like today, and they were often of a different ethnicity or race and sometimes living in a state other than the state where you know for sure your kin resided. There are times those with the same name are living in the same state, making it hard from time to time to determine when a person is one's ancestor and when he or she is not. So racial identifiers and knowing the place where the ancestor lived are extremely important.

The first census was taken in 1790. For most African Americans, it took sixty years for them to show up on the census documents with their names and other identifying information. Even then the African American as well as people of European and other nationalities had to be free inhabitants of this country to receive this mark of distinction. This occurred in 1870 for a lot of people who had been slaves and servants. If you find your ancestors in the census prior to 1870 with identifying information to include, but not limited to, age and race, then they were free either from the beginning of their existence or they had been freed before the Emancipation Proclamation.

The first US census was taken by US marshals on horseback in 1790, and they counted 3.9 million inhabitants at that time.[3] It is presumed that a portion of the census data for 1790 through 1830 was lost, making it hard to verify the numbers and any persons who were inhabitants, free or not, during those days. Research indicates that the 3.9 million inhabitants enumerated in 1790 included those who were slaves and listed only as a number under his or her master's name. Further research indicates that they were indeed counted as a full number in spite of the fact that slaves were not considered equals. Even so, to maintain the fact that servants and slaves were not as important as those who were white and not slaves or servants, such enumeration excluded the privilege of a name and other pertinent information. Such antics make it very hard for some of us to locate all our loved ones from the distant past, and these antics deprive us of the opportunity to pay homage to some of our ancestors if only by name.

Even today, the fight for equality continues as blatant attempts are made to exclude us from the privileges afforded other citizens. Still, attempts are made by some to block our votes. On a whole, our people are the last to be employed. Our neighborhoods are infested with drugs. But these have simply become annoying and aggravating attempts. Great progress has been made by many from the time of our arrival in this country, but not nearly enough for others.

Overall, we have gained greater courage to fight for our rights, and we know that there are laws to protect us as long as we are living properly. But you have to know that you know. Education is therefore very important, and so is a spiritual life. These are two of the most important keys to survival of a people. God says in Hosea 4:6, "My people are destroyed for lack of knowledge." I thank God for blessing me and my people with the wisdom of his Word and the precious blood of Jesus. I thank him for the comfort of the Holy Spirit.

Portals to my Soul

After researching and collecting personal family data that I have already shared with other family members, I decided I needed to open the portal to the souls of my family for others to read and to be able to use as a model in their individual quests. I realized that from the distant past and up to the present time, the souls of African Americans had to have been rooted in God to survive. I realized why a singer and songwriter Douglas Miller had the same opinion that so many of our people had yesterday and even have today. We had no choice but to have our souls anchored on the Lord. We actually needed to be spiritually rooted. In fact, the message here is when you have tried everything else in life and it hasn't worked and even before, you need to turn to and try Jesus. It is Jesus by way of the Father, the Almighty God, who gives us strength. All power comes from the Lord.

> Though the storms keep on raging in my life
> And sometimes it's hard to tell the night from day
> Still that hope that lies within is reassured
> As I keep my eyes upon the distant shores.[4]

So my interest expanded past the collection of family information and how we are related and who is who to what did my ancestors actually experience during this familial journey. In this document, you will find me attempting to connect the dots to what was actually occurring during those times. My family probably did not talk much about the struggling times because they probably knew the pain still felt even when they were successful. They also knew that if you focus on the negative, those things will create a life of their own and will grow at a rapid rate. John 6:63 tells us that our words are spirits. Mark 1:27 states that, even with authority, Jesus even commands the unclean spirits, and they do obey him. In other words, Jesus casted out the spirits with his words, and so can we. We can create good and bad things simply by speaking them. Words are spirits, and they are life. Thus saith the Lord.

Our Family Connections and other Generational Facts

Our family and others knew that we were related by blood to W. E. B. Du Bois and that we had French and West Indian ancestry. Over the years, I have been advised by my cousins of our Mandinka and Mende ancestry as well. We knew that classical music and opera as a profession and as an art were a part of our heritage on the Jackson/Frisby side and that some of our ancestors came from Madagascar on my maternal grandmother's maternal side, and I just learned somewhere in West Africa, probably Ghana, on my paternal grandmother's paternal side. I knew that my grandmother on the Moore side was one of thirty-four or more children from North Carolina with connections to Africa and possibly the beautiful island of Barbados. I knew about Odrick's Corner and its connection to the Hatcher and Odrick sides of the family. I knew a lot about these things, but not as much as I know now. My father had told us that we were mixed with quite a bit, and as always, he was right. We have a rich and diverse history.

But it is harder to trace our European and the probability of any Indian ancestry. At this time, such information is obscure. So for now, I am going to focus on those things I know and those things where there is clear evidence. We know that a few of our ancestors were from other than African descent due to the fact that they are listed in the census as mulatto. It is suspected that some of that mixture may have come from Europeans. On the other hand, there is a strong probability that our ancestors in Virginia may have mixed with other than the white population as well. Some of my ancestors could have in fact been triracial.

Anyway, as stated in the census, the terminology "mulatto" unfortunately did not take into consideration or determine the actual race or ethnicity of the person. The assistant marshall made this determination by visual appearances, which were unfolding in the mixed race people. The appearance of being mixed was the determining factor, and no conversation occurred as to the race or nationality of one's people. The full facts about these things may therefore never be uncovered. But what I know for sure is that we are African Americans. I know our people from Virginia and some of those born in Connecticut, Massachusetts, Pennsylvania, Maryland, and Washington DC and one of my greats in North Carolina were listed as mulatto when such terminology was being used for mixed people particularly for governmental tracking and tax purposes. After that, these same family members from both the North and the South were listed as Negro, colored or black.

We know about the French element in this case, but I have yet to uncover the other European or any Indian ancestries to the exact tribe or ethnicity. I do know that full-blooded Indians in the North were literally extinguished from constant battles with the European when the Indians were defeated and died rapidly from infectious diseases brought over to America from Europe. In addition, the Indian's land was negotiated and sold to the European for probably little or nothing. In many instances, after the sale of their land, Indians too were taken as slaves.

I know it is factual that, in many instances, the Indians mixed heavily with the Africans to the point where the Indian characteristics were no longer easily distinguishable as Indian. The African genes were obviously much stronger. It is the belief of many that very few full-blooded Indians are alive even today. They mixed heavily with the African and the white populations in this evolving country. Some of those with strong African characteristics remained tribal nevertheless. I also know that there were a lot of blacks who lived with and were allowed to identify themselves as black Indians. But I don't know for sure what occurred in my distant family. I do know that we do not personally identify with any Indian tribes or white ethnic groups. What I do know for sure is, we are African Americans.

But what did my ancestors really encounter during their compulsory trip from far lands of Africa to the eastern shores of America? What about the earlier times prior to and after the emancipation of my people? What was happening and how were my people treated and what was it like to be under the direct control of the white establishment and literally treated as inferior? Is it the same feeling that we feel today? I have a lot of questions, though I know such treatment had to have been drastic and probably unbearable. My ancestors had to have had the will to live, and they had to have had strong faith in God.

I actually want to know and so I am going to travel the eastern shores of America during the time when slavery was at its height and shortly thereafter when slavery was gradually dissipating and finally ended. I will stop in those places where I know for sure my ancestors were born and where they settled. It is for certain that they lived and remained on the East Coast of America, and they traveled from one place to another. These things will be the focus of my research. I will have to depend heavily on what I already know and what others have researched and documented to complete this journey.

New England Ancestry
New Haven County, Connecticut and
Massachusetts

I decided that my first stop on this soul journey would be New Haven, Connecticut, where my father and his sister and some of my ancient ancestors were born. Now that I know for sure who many of my souls are, I want to know what historical things were occurring back then and what history has to say about my people. I want to know exactly what they did to escape the snares of slavery and servitude and what and how much they sacrificed to ensure freedom for themselves and those who followed. For starters, I know that it was not only the African American who was in some sort of servitude, but so were others. Even an enormous number of those who were white were beholden to a master. But I want to know about my African American people. I want to know about their struggles and what they did to succeed and survive. I do know that there is nothing new under the sun especially since the same struggles are occurring today even with an African American president at the helm of this country. Things were different back then, but the results are basically the same. If nothing else, we have to admit that the masters back then were right about one thing all along. The African American vote would have indeed made a difference.

Unfortunately, most people of color have experienced some level of racism and discrimination in this country from time to time. However, in the earlier days, so many of our people experienced even more the thrash of the whip and hangings, verbal and physical threats and name-calling. But in spite of these harmful things, I am praying that the progressive and liberal whites continue to outnumber those who have yet to grow up and who do not know the God I know. If they did, we would not be having this conversation. Acts 10:34-35 clearly states that "God is no respecter of persons." It is my prayer that the abolitionists, the liberals, and the progressives will continue to be our allies like the Quakers who opposed slavery for a generation before the revolution. There was indubitably a spiritual conflict in American principles and human bondage going on during those times.

It is clear that the populations during those ancient times where my Northern ancestors dwelt in New York and New England were pretty miniscule, and even more so for African Americans. For this reason, it has been relatively easy to locate my lineage once on the right track. Wrong turns are expected, but they become quite obvious and debatable in your spirit. Trust in your spirit. You know when it is right because you feel the souls of your people. If you do err, just readjust and carry on.

New Haven's African American History

The first Europeans in New Haven, Connecticut, were supposedly the Dutch who established trade posts there.

By 1638 the English Puritans had settled in New Haven. The Puritans had hoped to gain freedom to practice religion as they saw fit, free from the corruption occurring in their churches. The Church of England had begun to focus too much on the needs of the aristocracy while oppressing the masses. Life in England was inflicted with opposing political and religious opinions. Numerous struggles and attacks were under way. King Charles I was beheaded. Those who opposed the political and religious changes occurring in their homeland established the Great Migration to America. This migration was in fact a reform movement. Thousands of English Puritans settled mainly in the New England colonies, Connecticut being one of them. Records indicate that this migration was short-lived and not very expansive and declined sharply for a while.[5] As in other places in America, the Indians already inhabited the territory in New Haven, which was settled by the Puritans, and it was the Indian's land that was taken or sold.

The Puritans in New Haven welcomed immigrants who were mainly from Poland and Italy. They were unskilled workers who were employed by the various factories located in the four largest cities in Connecticut, which included my hometown of Waterbury. These immigrants were crucial to Connecticut's growing economy. Moreover, these immigrants were Catholic and caused a shift in Connecticut's religious framework. Connecticut was historically a Protestant state. Connecticut's population was almost 30 percent immigrant by 1910.[6] The same article indicates that a significant number of Jewish immigrants also arrived in this period.

But it must be understood that immigration had and continues to have its purpose. Immigration is mostly about the economy and is still needed for economic reasons even today. In spite of any negative consequences, it appeared that life in this new country was better for various and sundry reasons. It mattered less that life in America was already being established as an exclusive regime. It was probably better than life in their homelands.

As for the African American in the earlier days, there was no choice. Being brought to this country as slaves was definitely by force. Even so, African Americans became a major part of this diaspora of various ethnicities onto the North American soil. And let us not forget that we were very instrumental in building this country. Without our cruel and unimaginable struggles, others would not have survived. But we like the Indians were deprived of our dignity and were treated as inferiors, and we were mostly enslaved. The establishment literally broke the backs of African Americans as well as the American Indians, and they murdered us at an alarming rate.

In spite of some African Americans carrying the title "free people of color," there were black laws that regulated an African American's comings and goings, free or not. Our presence in this country was by constraint, and we were brought here under cruel and unusual conditions, and we endured cruel and unusual punishment both on sea and on land. While some were free people of color employed as servants or farmworkers, others were slaves. Racism was rampant, and racism has continued throughout our existence in this country. This had been going on for quite a while though we have made tons and tons of progress when you look at the whole picture dating back to when the first slaves arrived in America.

In the early 1700s, records indicate that discrimination against free blacks was more severe in Connecticut than in other New England colony.[7] In addition, author Douglas Harper writes about the lives of African Americans and the application of the black laws in Connecticut. Basically, in 1690, the colony forbade blacks and Indians to be on the streets after a certain hour and African Americans had to carry a pass from their masters to wander past their town or boundaries. Whites and blacks had frequent fights, and the black man received the punishment. Even speech was subject to control;

and this law applied to a black, Indian, or mulatto slave who uttered or published unacceptable words about a white person. The black, Indian, or mulatto slave was whipped with forty lashes, if convicted.[8]

African Americans who were free in New Haven and other places in and around the early and midnineteenth century owned property and paid taxes, but their rights were limited to the same rights as those who were slaves. In other words, they had no other rights. Even the federal government at this time did not consider free African Americans to be full citizens. They were prohibited from carrying the federal mail or from holding public office. They could not vote. In addition, in spite of the fact that African Americans played a significant role in the American Revolution, they were excluded from the postwar national militia. To add to this, early naturalization laws that were in place at the time were reserved for white aliens only.[9]

According to the writings of Alice Mick and Lula White whose writings on African Americans in New Haven and those of others on this topic cover quite a bit of ground, lawyers, clergyman, and merchants controlled the development of the laws of New Haven. They practiced bigotry and hatred toward others who were not like them and that included the Italians who were viewed as inferior. In fact, these individuals who had power over the community at large disallowed African Americans to be buried in the same area of the cemeteries as others. It mattered not that an African American was free. There were clearly attempts to keep African Americans in a state of serfdom and in poverty and separated from the community at large. Many African Americans were paupers who searched for jobs and a better life. Agriculture and trade were initially the primary sources of employment in Connecticut, but land in New Haven was scarce and the inhabitants had to come up with new ways of making money as more people migrated to the State. Industrialization seemed to be the answer, and in the early 1800s, manufacturing began to expand into various areas of employment that were once handled manually. Still, African Americans in New Haven were blocked from engaging in any employment that would have assisted them in becoming prosperous or at least respected.

Many African Americans who relocated to New Haven originated from the rural areas of the North or from the South in search of manual labor. But lack of skills and closed doors made it impossible for them to succeed at the same rate as others. According to Mick and White, those who migrated from the South were mainly from Newbern, North Carolina. Newbern is located in North Carolina's Inner Banks region. The initial settlers in Newbern were Swiss and German immigrants. The African American migrants from the South were masons and carpenters and blacksmiths. They were also waiters and barbers and seaman.[10] Still, most of our ancestors in New Haven migrated from other northern places. In spite of their skills, gainful employment for African Americans was quickly overtaken by those who emigrated from Italy to America.

I must point out that the Jackson seed may have originated in New Haven, and they may have or may not have been free. My cousin Katherine Jackson Harris who is a native of New Haven and has been so all her life, which is eighty-five years, advised me that I had not taken the Jackson ancestry in America far enough back. For instance, there is a cemetery plot for our Jackson family in New Haven that goes back to the sixteenth or seventeenth century. She informed me that one of our ancient ancestors, William Jackson, is buried there, and he died in the 1700s. Also, a member of the Jackson family was an appointee to one of the black governors of Connecticut.

New Haven had three black governors between 1825 through 1837. Connecticut had allowed African Americans to elect their own governors during this time. These governors were raised from the black communities, and their purpose was to help whites maintain control over the black people. Ironically, black governors could still be enslaved while serving. In essence, these black officials served as mediators between the white establishment and the communities of blacks, and they handed out punishment to slaves who violated the laws.[11]

My cousin further states that our Jackson family originally gathered and remained in and around the New Haven area, and mainly in New Haven where my father was born. I have in fact discovered that Hempstead, Long Island, New York, is another place of ancestral significance for the Jackson seed. I do know that territorial disputes occurred regarding whether Connecticut or New York actually possessed Long Island. This dispute was resolved in 1664 when Long Island was granted to New York.

Our relatives must have been traveling back and forth between New Haven and Long Island. Some settled in New Haven and others in New York. So eventually I will have to study these developments and search many years earlier to try to identify our ancestors from the late sixteenth and early seventeenth centuries. I do know for sure that my third great-grandparents Semon and Leonora Jackson were born in Hempstead, New York, in about 1787 and their children and some of their grandchildren were born there as well. I was unable to determine the names and birthplaces of their parents who would have been my fourth great-grandparents.

The Housing Issue in New Haven

Housing was another issue that confronted the African America in New Haven. Boundaries were established, and the main area for African Americans to live in New Haven was named Sodom Hill, eventually shortened to the Hill. Mick and White state that this area extended "out along Negro Lane, now State Street, which was supposedly a better section of town for blacks, and ran along lower Dixwell Avenue." Dixwell Avenue is where my grandmother lived since the late 1940s. Prior to and during the early 1920s, my grandfather and grandmother lived at 74 Edgewood Avenue in New Haven and then at 87 Admiral Street. They lived just streets away from Dixwell Avenue and Whalley and Sherman Avenues and the North Frontage Road in this African American community but also not far from Yale. Today, the western central neighborhood, which includes Dixwell and the neighborhood on the south end of the city, continues to have basically the same community structure.

My grandfather was a student at Yale and was a member of Yale's 1919 class. He enrolled in 1915 and attended Yale for a couple of years, studying and running track, but he did not complete his education there. He met my grandmother, who was one of Yale's first African American secretaries, and he evidently fell in love with her. I can understand his love for her. She was beautiful, and had a smooth caramel color with long wavy hair. They married in 1916 and started their family in 1917. He was employed by the Greist Manufacturing Company as a clerk in 1917 and then he worked for the United States Post Office. In 1930, he is located in Haverford, Delaware County, Pennsylvania, divorced and working as a butler for Thorpe Nesbit, Esq. Granddaddy lived in the Nesbit home for a while.

In or around 1940, Esquire Nesbit must have moved his practice to Philadelphia or maybe he was already working there. My grandfather worked in his business or his home as a chauffeur, I am told. The firm was located at 1240 Land Title Building in Philadelphia. My grandfather lived in Philadelphia. I am also told that an attorney who was a close friend of my grandfather paid the total cost of my father's education at Lincoln University. This could have been Esquire Nesbit.

My grandfather was a character and loved having fun. I have pictures of him with the maids that worked with him in Haverford and maybe Philadelphia as well. I also have pictures of him with members of the Thorpe Nesbit's family to include Thorpe Sr., his wife, Edith, and their children Hope and Thorpe Jr. Granddaddy and Thorpe Nesbit were very close in age, and he very much respected my grandfather to the point where they probably became very close friends.

In the 1930s, Attorney Nesbit had acquired some assets but was still renting his home. Martha Pittman was a little younger and worked as a maid, along with Lucille Thomas, both African Americans. Also, working in this private household was Mary Scott, the white governess who was employed to teach and train the two children. Granddaddy and the two maids appeared to love their working environment, and there appeared to be a close bond among everyone. Granddaddy is often at the beach or at outings with his African American male and female friends, and they appear extremely happy, and they were stunningly dressed. I am not surprised. You can only have fun around Granddaddy.

African American Communities in New Haven

Whalley, Goffe, and Sperry Streets were major thoroughfares surrounding this African American community. Three of these streets were named after the judges who had signed the death warrant of Charles I in England. They were Colonel Edward Whalley, Colonel William Goffe, and John Dixwell. Based on their signing of the death warrant, these three judges were pursued by Charles II, the son to Charles I. As a result, these three regicides fled to America, specifically New Haven, for refuge. Sperry Street was named after Richard Sperry who was an antiroyalist who aided and abetted the judges who had a death warrant over their heads. They hid in the Judge Caves in New Haven on the West Rocks. I don't know what eventually happened to them, but I do know they were important enough to have streets named after them.

My grandmother's brother, great-uncle Alexander Jackson, lived at 343 Munson Street not far from his sister in the community where a number of African Americans in New Haven resided and even reside today. As much as things change, they remain the same. Yale University, which makes up much of New Haven's current economy, is located not far from this area.[12] Yale-New Haven Hospital and the Yale School of Medicine border a residential area where crime, poverty, and drugs, at least as I recall, remain problems. I remember having to pass through this neighborhood and crossing the immediate dividing line with Yale when I would be en route to the railroad station. According to records about New Haven, attempts to erase this inequity and unfairness go back as far as the 1800s.

National Crisis during Slavery Rebellions and Revolts

Now within time, a revelation occurred to some of the Congregationalist ministers in New Haven that slavery was not fair and should therefore be abolished. The liberalists or abolitionists fought to make life better for the African American, or Negro or mulatto, whatever name is most preferred. I prefer African American, and I will use this terminology to describe my people of color throughout this document though other terminologies may be used for emphasis. During these earlier years, an attempt was made to start an African American school, and this action was intermingled with other undertakings needed to equalize the African American at that time. As you can imagine, this idea was met with much resistance, and the thought of it clearly frightened the white man. They knew if a person or a people became educated, they will begin to know what is what, and they will learn to be creative in their thinking and may even gain power over their lives. The majority of the white ruling force felt that such a thing could not be allowed to happen.

Two major African American incidents occurred during this time that would have reasonably frightened the white man even more and would have dissuaded any thought of integration. Nat Turner, a slave, plotted a revolt in Southampton County, Virginia, in August 1831. This revolt was later referred to as the "Southampton Insurrection" or, more frequently, "Nat Turner's Rebellion." He and his comrades killed close to fifty-seven white people who were more likely uncompassionate slave owners and their family members who had made the slaves' lives quite miserable and intolerable. Nat Turner was a Baptist preacher who had significant influence among the black slaves, and because of this, he easily led this rebellion.[13] He was caught and executed by hanging along with others who participated in this revolt.

Later in 1839, the Amistad revolt occurred where fifty-three Africans were abducted by the Spanish slave trade from Sierra Leone, a safe haven for freed slaves. A revolt led by a twenty-six-year old man Cinqué, who was among the captured from Mende, Sierra Leone, resulted in a landmark decision by the United States Supreme Court in which the court ruled in favor of the African rebels. New Haven was the place where the Mende revolutionists were jailed due to this mutiny, and their trial was held in New Haven's United States District Court. Currently, there is a statue of Joseph Cinqué beside City Hall in recognition of this landmark ruling.

Tradition has it that my ancient Mende ancestors were more than likely a part of this Amistad revolt and its accompanying landmark decision. The population was so small in New Haven and other areas of America during this time. The African American population was even smaller. So those who revolted probably had relatives who were brought over as slaves before them. Our Northern family's DNA shows both Mandinka and Mende heritage. If tradition holds true, some of my ancestors who were aboard that ship were brought to trial in New Haven and, more importantly, had won the first civil rights case in America. These types of gains were few and far between. But in spite of this landmark decision and in spite of our ancestor's hard work, African Americans were denied the right to vote or to swim in public pools or to sit with dignity in the white man's church pews or to attend their schools. I continue to wonder why the right to vote or be educated was such a grave concern at the time. But it seems as though God had a different plan.

But these were not the only revolts. Slaves were known to revolt throughout the various decades in which slavery existed. My recent research revealed that they revolted more than I had ever imagined, and they had quite a bit of support to help them gain their freedom. If it had not been for the faith and fortitude of the slaves, we would not have been able to endure as a people. We would have become relatively extinct pretty much like the full-blooded Indian has in the Northeast and in other places. If it had not been for the fact that there is a God who gave us his Son, we would not have been able to survive. Faith helped our people to bear the burden of slavery, not to give up and to keep our focus and hope on better times. Through faith, we learned to ride on and through the raging storms.

And then there was Denmark Vesey, a free African American, who planned a revolt, but he and his thirty men were hanged before their plan was carried out. There had already been similar revolts as early as 1712. On April 6, 1712, slaves killed nine whites in the New York Slave Revolt and an unknown number of African Americans died in this uprising.[14]

Times in slavery were not as complacent as they may have seemed. The slaves exhibited quite a bit of resistance to slavery which is quite understandable. There were a lot of attempts throughout the early 1700s and into the late 1800s toward gaining freedom and equality or merely enjoying the simple pleasures of life. Times were so bad during slavery that slaves in a lot of places couldn't even officially marry and their children were labeled as illegitimate. That is how bad things were for the African American. So they jumped the broom as a seal and symbol of their love and commitment to each other.

Antislavery movements seemed to be rapidly increasing as slaves became really tired and disenchanted with their unfair and inhumane bondage. What else could one expect from a caged human? Also, in the late nineteenth century, the landmark Dred Scott decision resulted in a lot of unrest among African Americans. African American protests were increasing due to the fugitive slave law passed by Congress in 1885. Basically, the Supreme Court's decision was that Dred Scott was still a slave in spite of him living for years outside of a slave state with his master's consent. As a result of the Dred Scott ruling, more and more African Americans were in favor of African colonization. Either integrate and free us or allow us to segregate seemed to be the message. To add fuel to the fire, Chief Justice Roger B. Taney concluded that African Americans, slave or free, were not citizens of the United States and were not entitled to the protections of the Constitution.[15] The battle for freedom and civil rights continued and so did white support in favor of freedom for the African American. Unlike their counterparts, the white supporters had loving souls. God bless them.

Connecticut's Gradual Emancipation of its Slaves

By 1784, the State of Connecticut passed the Gradual Emancipation Act of 1784. This resulted from the efforts of the abolition forces. These forces tactically compromised with the opposition to free African Americans from human bondage. They actually presented a bill to the legislature for gradual emancipation. This bill or rider was presented as part of a statute that codified race relations. It provided that black and mulatto children born after March 1 would become free at age twenty-five. Their strategy worked, and the bill passed with little or no opposition. Eventually, the age was reduced to twenty-one. But after the established time was served, the ex-slaves received no support and no professional standing and were basically left to fend for themselves. As in other Northern states, "gradual emancipation freed no slaves at once. It simply set up slavery for a long-term natural death." Connecticut finally abolished slavery entirely in 1848.[16]

Shortly thereafter, African Americans were free to establish their own institutions in New Haven. Yet they continued to be banned from attending white schools, churches, and other social institutions. When they were allowed to attend the white church, they were publicly ridiculed and reduced to the lowest self-esteem. But a push by the most liberal whites to establish separate institutions for African Americans in the New Haven area was successful. That was the most they could do to contribute to the right of African Americans to hold their heads high with dignity and pride. For African Americans to enjoy at least similar privileges, separate institutions appeared to be the first step toward total freedom.

Integration was clearly out of the question for those in power during those times, and there was little flexibility to give African Americans any power, dignity, equal rights, or respect. But in spite of it all, African Americans organized segregated churches, businesses, schools, and organizations owned and controlled by them and for their purpose and for their growth.

By 1850, the joint efforts of some white sympathizers and some strong-minded African Americans resulted in the continued formation of three New Haven schools for African Americans. The first African American school in New Haven opened in 1811.[17] It goes without saying that these schools were mournfully substandard, extremely mediocre, and to a greater extent, just downright inadequate for learning. But we must understand that we had to start somewhere. I wonder if my ancestors were part of the newly formed school, New Goffe Street School, in 1865, or those established prior to this particular one.

My third great-grandparents were Alexander Dubois (b. 1803 and d. 1887) and the former Sarah Marsh Lewis (b. 1804 and d. 9 July 1834). They married on 4 May 1823 more than likely in New Haven. We already know that third great-grandfather Alexander was born in the Bahamas and attended a gentleman's school in Cheshire. Third great-grandmother Sarah probably was born in New Haven, Connecticut, where she and third great-grandfather Alexander lived. Third great-grandmother Sarah would have been of school age in 1811 when the first African American school was founded, and she may have attended school during that time. We do know that around this time third great-grandfather Alexander was enrolled in a gentleman's school in Cheshire. They were free people of color as were their children.

One of their children, Henry A. Dubois, was born 26 February 1825, and he married Sarah A. Brown, born in 1827. They were my second great-grandparents, and they both were born and raised in New Haven. Most, if not all, of their children were born in Cheshire, Connecticut, with the oldest born in 1848 and the youngest, my great-grandmother Nettie A. Dubois, born in 1871. But some of my Dubois family members, particularly the other children born to my third great-grandparents, Alexander and Sarah Dubois, may have remained in New Haven during this period of time.

I tried to trace some of the other children, sisters, and brothers to my second great-grandfather and found three possibilities from those Dubois members who were born in New Haven and were listed as black or mulatto as follows: Benjamin Dubois (b. abt. 1827), Diana Dubois (b. abt. 1828), John Dubois (b. abt. 1828), and possibly others. My second great-grandfather Henry may have attended one of the first schools since he was living in New Haven at the time, and education held high standards with his father, third great-grandfather Alexander, and probably his mother as well.

By 1850, my second great-grandparents Henry A. Dubois and the former Sarah A. Brown had moved to Cheshire, Connecticut. In fact, second great-grandfather Henry is listed in the 1850 census as living with his wife, my second great-grandmother, Sarah A. Brown Dubois, in Cheshire as free inhabitants with two children who appear to be twins. All four are listed as born in Connecticut. So there is a strong possibility that my second great-grandparents were in the New Haven schools when at least the first school had been established. Since Cheshire was not that far away, some of their younger children who would have been of school age could have attended one of the schools as well or went to school in Cheshire at least for a few years. My great-grandmother Nettie who was their youngest child is listed in the census as having attended school, and she is able to read and write.

Records indicate that, by 1869, there were more than two hundred African Americans enrolled in New Haven's segregated schools.[18] But African American parents objected to this racial separation in the educational system, which forced their children into an inferior school setting. They insisted that their children be educated in the finer schools restricted to whites only. As one can only imagine, there was quite an alarming difference in the two educational systems. The pressure for change eventually worked but mostly at a slow rate. Most change does not happen overnight anyway. With the civil war ending and the subsequent passage of the Fifteenth Amendment, the legislated segregation of schools in New Haven gradually ended, and in 1874, the last separate school on Goffe Street was officially closed.[19]

At this particular time in history, African American children were allowed and did attend public schools that were previously reserved for whites only. All this seemed to have occurred after my second and third great-grandparents' residency in New Haven at least on the Dubois side, which is a major part of our ancestry on my father's paternal side. Census records indicate that third great-grandfather Alexander Dubois had moved from Connecticut to Massachusetts and his son, my second great-grandfather, Henry, to Cheshire, Connecticut.

But one or more of the progenitors on the Jackson side could have very easily been a part of this changing phenomenon to integrate the schools, and they also may have attended one of the African American schools before schools were integrated in New Haven. The Jackson family members were my great-grandparents on my father's maternal side. Great-grandfather Robert H. Jackson was born in 1863 in New Haven, Connecticut, to William and Henrietta Jackson who were both born in Hempstead, New York. Great-grandfather Robert would have been six years old at the time of the creation of at least one of the African American schools in New Haven. His sister Henrietta would have been ten years old and his brother Benjamin eleven years old. So even though the Dubois family may have moved away by 1865, members of the Jackson side of the family were born and lived in New Haven at the time of the educational dilemma. They lived in ward 1 not far from Yale. Now that I think about it, they must have experienced these altering and life-changing events.

Great-grandfather Robert eventually lived at 94 Eaton Street about four miles from Dixwell Avenue, and he was listed as black unlike a lot of my other paternal ancestors to include his wife, my great-grandmother, Madame Henrietta Frisby Jackson, who were listed as mulatto. He worked as a messenger and at some point was employed as a steward at the Elks Club both in Rutland, Vermont and in New Haven, Connecticut. My aunt Natalie just informed me that my cousin Bruce Jackson is an identical image of his grandfather who was my great-grandfather, Robert H. Jackson.

As stated earlier, some of my Dubois ancestors, at least my second and third great-grandparents, left the city of New Haven. My second great-grandfather Henry A. Dubois moved to

Cheshire, Connecticut, which was in proximity to New Haven and is part of New Haven County, and my third great-grandfather Alexander moved further north to Massachusetts. Also, as stated previously, second great-grandfather Henry is listed in the 1850 census as a free inhabitant, and he is living with my second great-grandmother Sarah and two small children in Cheshire. In the 1870 census he and his family continued to live in Cheshire, and he is listed as a laborer and two of his fourteen children at the time who were young adults were listed as farmers. After this census, they had another child born in 1871 who was my great-grandmother Nettie. Second great-grandfather Henry A. Dubois obviously followed his father's footsteps toward economic freedom. He was already a free inhabitant and had always been free.

While in New Haven, third great-grandfather Alexander Dubois owned a grocery store on 23 Washington Street in New Haven, Connecticut. He also worked on the New York-New Haven boat line that ferried passengers between New York and New Haven, Connecticut. As these boats traveled northward from Suffolk County to Connecticut, third great-grandfather Alexander fought for the rights of African Americans who were treated improperly aboard these boats. His grocery store, and possibly his home as well, were located near Lafayette Street and Congress Avenue south of the S. Frontage Road in the African American section of town. It was located less than half a mile from the center area of the Hill, and not far from what is now Yale-New Haven Hospital. The New Haven City directory published in the mideighteen hundreds lists the names and occupations of others living or with businesses in close proximity to third great-grandfather Alexander and his family. Other than third great-grandfather, they were listed as white and their occupations were as follows: shoemaker, cabinet and lamp makers, harness maker, ship master, carriage trimmer, meat marketer, stone ware manufacturer, teachers, clerks, barber and painter, among other occupations. Based on this and other city directories, third great-grandfather Alexander was still living in New Haven in 1847 and 1848.

From the 1850 census forward third great-grandfather Alexander is living in Massachusetts—first in Springfield, then Agawam, Hamden, Massachusetts, where he owned property valued at $4,000, which equates to $200,000 in today's currency, and he also had some personal assets. Before his death, he is listed in New Bedford, Bristol, Massachusetts, at 93 Acushnet Avenue, which is a home I am more than sure he owned as well. Records indicate he arrived in Massachusetts in or around 1850. Prior to then he lived in New Haven where he was instrumental in coestablishing an African American church, St. Luke's Episcopal Church. This church still stands today.

Cheshire, Connecticut

In Cheshire, New Haven County, Connecticut, second great-grandfather Henry A. Dubois worked hard to support his family. In 1850, he is definitely living in Cheshire as a grown man with his wife and two children at the time. They ended up having fifteen children: James (b. 1847), Sarah (b. 1848), Joseph (b. 1851), George Walter (b. 1852), Charlotte P. (b. 1855), Louisa (b. 1858), Eugene (b. 1860), Jennie (b. 1861), Thomas (b. 1862), John (b. 1865), Julia (b. 1865), Sarah Louise (b. 1866), Mary Jane (b. 1868), Charlie (b. 1869) and Nettie (b. 1871). Second great-grandfather Henry was a laborer in those days. I was unable to locate for whom he may have worked. Tax records for 1863 and 1866 are readily available and contain his taxable income and any personal assets, but not his employer.

In 1863, second great-grandfather Henry had a household income of $5,730.00 taxed at 3 percent, which equated to a tax amount of $171.93 on his income. He had other assets worth $603.00, which were also taxable. Those assets included one carriage with one horse, another carriage with two horses, and a plate of silver. Quite a few white retail dealers lived in the Cheshire area, and they had also acquired a substantial amount of property and assets. In today's dollars, second great-grandfather Henry would have had an annual income and net worth of $116,432.23.[20]

In 1866, his income and assets increased significantly as it appears he was working two jobs. As usual, the names of the employers were not listed on the assessor's tax rolls. But his taxable income was listed in the 1866 tax records and his income was $54,410.00. His estimated income would be $840,705.89 in today's dollars. He owned other taxable property: two carriages, three horses, two gold watches, a piano, and a silver plate with a combined value of $5,545.00, which equates to $85,677.52 in today's dollars. In 1866, his total worth and income was $59,955, which would be $926,383.41 in today's dollars. Second great-grandfather Henry was acquiring wealth at an accelerated rate, and he was nowhere near a pauper. In fact, if his income continued at this rate or greater, he would be among the wealthy men of his time. But my second great-grandparents had fifteen children and a lot of mouths to feed, though probably not all at one time. Some of the children were approaching adulthood, and at least one died at a young age. Nevertheless, second great-grandfather Henry definitely benefited from the burgeoning economy in the Northeast.

Second great-grandfather Henry A. Dubois's picture that remained all these years in the home where I was raised shows him as a buff individual who probably had to have been strong to work the laborious tasks that he did. He looked to be of full size and mighty strong, though he may not have been very tall. He was fashionably dressed. Records indicate he had two sources of income in 1866 and may have worked for two employers or had at least profits from a farm that he may have owned. He might have helped to build and maintain the canals or he may have loaded the docks. Attempts at improving the movement of goods along the rivers and stream were under way a little prior to his move to Cheshire. And so the Farmington Canal was in operation and millions of pounds of merchandise were shipped every month from New Haven through Hamden, Cheshire, Southington, Bristol, Farmington, Simsbury, and Granby, bound for Northampton, Massachusetts, on the Farmington Canal.[21]

More and more products were being produced outside the home and in mills and factories. Industrialization was at its prime. Waterways were the key to internal transportation and were important to the building of the economy. Other possibilities that could have served as employment for second great-grandfather Henry would have been working on the development of the turnpikes, or he could have worked on the railroad. The railroad replaced the canals as canal usage diminished, and the railroads became more desirable. The railroad was a much faster method for transporting goods and less dangerous. Other transportation at that time included steamboats and rafts, horses and mules, carriages and stagecoaches, and oxen, to name a few. Rivers and streams and the railroad system were key elements in the transportation of coal and products made of iron and steel, which were major industries in this area.

Second great-grandfather could have also worked in the factories where buttons and clocks were manufactured in Cheshire, or he could have been a silversmith in Wallingford. Wallingford and Cheshire were once combined. Another option was that he may have worked in Cheshire's stone industry. During this time, a mineral was discovered called Barite, which was used largely in the painting industry. During a period of forty years in the nineteenth century, about 160,000 tons of white barite was mined at Cheshire, Connecticut.[22] Wherever he worked as a laborer, he was definitely contributing to the economy.

He had to have been a very hard worker, and he had to have been very intelligent since he was successful in building his own wealth.

Second great-grandfather Henry was listed as a free inhabitant and may have had a heavy French-Bahamian accent causing the US Marshall who took the census to spell the surname, and sometimes even the first name, the way it was obviously spoken. Of course, this resulted in the surname being spelled incorrectly. Also, the poor handwriting of the US Marshall caused some information to be illegible. When his older sons, James and Joseph, became of age in the 1870 census, they were listed as farmers. So at some point they probably owned their own land. Wherever second great-grandfather Henry worked, he was successful and is currently noted as a member of "Cheshire's Black Community." Finally, Cheshire had a few slaves and servants, but he was not one of them. He was a free inhabitant. He died on 9 November 1892 from pneumonia.

New Haven Pioneers

Returning to the city of New Haven, the doors of opportunity began to open for African Americans to study and earn degrees from Yale College, now Yale University. The Yale African American Affinity Group lists several African American pioneers who studied at Yale in the 1800s. These pioneers set the stage and made it possible for other African Americans to attend and study at Yale. These pioneers included the first attendee who was a fugitive slave as well as the first African American to receive his doctorate from an American university.[23]

My paternal grandfather, Theodore W. Hatcher Sr., attended Yale in approximately 1915 and was a member of the class of 1919. He may have been interested in studying law. I am told he was a track star at Yale as well. My grandmother, the former Romietta Leonora

Jackson, was one of the first African American secretaries employed by Yale. My sister, Dr. Barbara J. Hatcher, did her clinical studies at Yale while a student at the University of Connecticut at Storrs. At least one other member of the Dubois clan, Charlotte Dubois, also appears to have attended Yale. She was one of the children born to third great-grandfather Alexander and his second wife, the former Mary Emily Jacklyn.

My grandparents, Theodore and Romietta, married in 1916 and had two children—my aunt, the former Natalie Roberta Hatcher, and my father, Theodore William Hatcher Jr. My grandfather was born in Waterbury, Connecticut, to Henry A. Hatcher originally from Fairfax County, Virginia, and Nettie A. Dubois, born in Cheshire, Connecticut. She was daughter to Henry A. Dubois and Sarah A. Brown Dubois who were both born in New Haven, Connecticut, and she was one of fifteen children. Great-grandmother Nettie was a grandchild to Alexander Dubois as was W. E. B. Du Bois. They did not have the same parents and had only one grandparent in common and that was third great-grandfather Alexander Dubois. Great-grandmother Nettie's grandmother was the former Sarah Marsh Lewis while W. E. B. Du Bois's grandmother was an unknown woman from Haiti. Nevertheless, they were first cousins to the half degree and their fathers, Henry and Alfred, respectively, were half brothers. From here forward, I will drop the halves as much as possible, and I will only use it for clarification of relationships. I never embraced this identifier even when I was young. It is my strong opinion that either you are related or you are not.

I am relatively, but not totally, sure that great-grandma Nettie and WEB may have never met each other, or if they did, it was brief. Based on WEB's writings, it is somewhat apparent that after his father Alfred and his mother Mary Burghardt Dubois divorced, his father Alfred left Massachusetts and settled in Milford, Connecticut.

More than likely WEB's family in Massachusetts may have severed any ties to the other Dubois members to include those raised and born in Connecticut. What a shame. I wanted very badly to know WEB. But I have always felt his soul as though I knew him. I was and continue to be impressed with his intellect and his courage. Ironically, I was interested in the sociological aspect of life just as he was without even knowing this beforehand. WEB was actually my first cousin, three times removed. Also, one of the professors who wrote the introduction to WEB's book *The Souls of Black Folks*, was one of my sociology professors at Howard University. His name is Dr. Nathan Hare.

"And these are they which are sown on good ground; such as hear the word, and receive it, and bring forth fruit, some thirtyfold, some sixty, and some an hundred" (Mark 4:20).

African American Spiritual Accomplishments

Not only was there a major push in New Haven to educate the African American, but a proper spiritual life, or lack thereof, was also of major concern. The period from 1820 to 1860 witnessed the beginning of numerous African American congregations in New Haven.[24] The first African American church was known as the Temple Street Church and later as the Dixwell Avenue Congregational Church.[25] It was also referred to as Dixwell Avenue United Church of Christ. This church has an illustrious history. This is the church that my aunt Natalie, the former Natalie Roberta Hatcher, has attended since 1927 when she was ten years old. She attended Sunday school and participated in the youth group activities offered at this church. Founded in 1820, this church describes itself as having engaged in ministry, activism, and fellowship throughout its 189 years working to better the lives of its members and the local and Christian community.[26]

History captures the fact that in 1820, Simeon Jocelyn and twenty-four former slaves organized the African Ecclesiastical Society. As a white abolitionist, Mr. Jocelyn demonstrated the passion and commitment necessary to lead this congregation. The society would meet at various homes throughout New Haven until establishing itself on Temple Street and Mr. Jocelyn served as the first minister. The church moved to 100 Dixwell Avenue and then moved to its current location under the leadership of Reverend Dr. Edwin R. Edmonds at the time.[27]

Aunt Natalie has been a member of this church for years. She sang in the Senior Choir since 1948 and also sang with the Joyful Praise Choir. She served as Sunday schoolteacher and served on various church committees. A former choir director and organist at her church described her as "a singer extraordinaire" and the church loft has been dedicated in her honor.[28] She received other recognitions and honorable mentions from her church. But before that, Aunt Natalie and her brother Theodore, my father, were christened at St. Luke's Episcopal Church that was cofounded by their second great-grandfather Alexander Dubois in 1844. They may not have known this at the time and it didn't seem to surface in discussions until years later and in more detail recently during my interviews with Aunt Natalie. She was pretty sure about our ancestors, but didn't know to what extent we were related. She asked me to find the link and then to inform the St. Luke's Episcopal Church accordingly. I hope this book serves her request accordingly.

My grandmother, Romietta Leonora Jackson, was born in Oakland, California, but lived more than eighty-five years in New Haven, Connecticut. She was a long-time member of St. Luke's Episcopal Church. I believe from this church she was eulogized. Her father, Robert H. Jackson, and her brother, Alexander Jackson, were born in New Haven, Connecticut, and her mother in Washington

DC. New Haven, Connecticut, was Grandma Ro's home, and she lived there in the African American community in the Dixwell area and mainly on Dixwell Avenue for a great majority of her life.

Paradoxically, not until I conducted this research and received a copy of my father's birth certificate from my mother was I aware of Grandma Ro's place of birth. I had always assumed that New Haven, Connecticut, was her place of birth, but both my father and aunt definitely knew otherwise. The reason why Grandma was in Oakland, California, at the time of her birth has finally unfolded. I am told that Grandma Ro's father had remained east at that particular time. So he was not in Oakland when Grandma was born. But shortly after Grandma Ro's birth, she is located in the 1900 census in Rutland, Vermont, where her father's occupation is listed as a steward at the Elks Club. Her mother's occupation is listed as a singer. My great-grandparents Robert and Henrietta and my grandmother eventually moved back to New Haven where her brother Alexander Jackson was born.

Grandma Ro's mother, Madame Henrietta Frisby Jackson, was an opera singer and an understudy for Sissieretta Jones, who was also referred to as Black Patti, and she was a member of Mme. Sissieretta's troupe. Great-grandmother Henrietta performed with Madame Sissieretta Jones in California's Bay area. A newspaper advertisement in the "San Francisco Call" dated February 3, 1989, announced the first appearance of the Black Patti Troubadours at the California Theatre. Operatic reviews were a part of her performances as well as vaudeville, comedy, cakewalks, and jubilee shouts, to name a few. Great-grandmother Henrietta was one of the singers in the troupe. As an understudy, she probably traveled many places with Sissieretta during her performances in other countries and several places in the United States to include Madison Square Garden and Carnegie Hall in New York. She more than likely was with Sissieretta when she performed before four presidents in Washington DC. Records indicate that Sissieretta Jones traveled the world performing mainly for white audiences. She even performed in London before the Prince of Wales.[29]

Sissieretta's operatic talents and performances were ultimately combined with the black vaudeville stage. During the Jim Crow era, African American artists created this type of entertainment to open up more opportunities for black performers. Whites supported this type of entertainment. Great-grandmother Henrietta continued as an understudy and a member of the troupe, and she may have had additional skills with designing and sewing costumes. After all, in addition to the musical selections, a performer's wardrobe is very crucial to the overall performance. Again, the operatic reviews continued even in this venue. In conclusion, Great-grandmother Henrietta was in the California bay area performing with Sissieretta at the time of my grandmother's birth, and she is listed in the census as a singer. She, like other opera singers, referred to herself as "Madame."

Research indicates that Oakland was one of the major depots in the west, and Rutland, Vermont, where my great-grandparents were living, was a major depot connecting the northeast to the west. America's transcontinental railroad linked California to the rest of the country and allowed for the transportation of agricultural goods from state to state. Travel to California was encouraged during those days and the railroads were the first to promote California tourism. San Francisco had been a major destination.

Paris of the West: Grandmother Ro's Birthplace

My grandmother was born in Oakland in 1899. During the late 1890s, San Francisco was becoming one of America's big cities and became a regular stop for great singers and touring companies. San Francisco was often referred to as the Paris of the West. Also, African American opera singers were touring the world in the late nineteenth century, and the female opera singer referred to herself as "Madame."[30] There were definitely a few African Americans in the mix among the Bay area artists and performers. So my great-grandmother, Madame Henrietta Frisby Jackson, ended up in an Oakland hospital where she birthed her first child while on tour with Sissieretta in the San Francisco Bay area. An African American concert singer had great opportunities in the San Francisco Bay Area and the Bay area continues to be a great venue for artists even today.

Who was Sissieretta Jones? She was born Matilda Sissieretta Joyner Jones in Portsmouth, Virginia (b. 1869, d. 1933). Posters created for her performances described her as "the Black Patti: Mme. M. Sissieretta Jones, the Greatest Singer of her Race." But Sissieretta vehemently objected to being called "the Black Patti." This title was used to describe her talents, which were considered equal to that of the celebrated Italian soprano Adelina Patti.[31] This occurred during the Jim Crow days, and her objections did not seem to mean a thing. She is described by the Library of Congress as a remarkable soprano voice and a commanding presence that won her personal success. She was highly decorated for her professional triumphs, and she performed at the White House for President Benjamin Harrison and in London before the Prince of Wales. She performed in opera houses and on the vaudeville stage. Records indicate that her success paved the way for other African Americans artists.[32]

Great-grandmother Henrietta's daughter, my Grandma Ro, was a renowned classical pianist well-known in New Haven and my grandmother's daughter, Aunt Natalie, was an opera singer, and she followed the footsteps of her grandmother, Mme. Henrietta Frisby Jackson. Grandma Ro often accompanied her daughter at many of her singing engagements. We visited them quite often at 68 Dixwell Avenue when we were children. Aunt Natalie and her husband, Uncle Rowland Douglas, lived at 66 Dixwell Avenue. Sometimes we were in attendance at Aunt Natalie's concerts and performances. Grandma Ro was so well-read and so extremely sophisticated. We didn't play around in her immaculately-kept home. When our family visited with Grandma, my sisters and I would listen, read, and learn. She had a lot of books and magazines, and her den was set up like a library, and it was equally serene. She commanded respect just because of who she was and how she related to people.

Aunt Natalie was blessed with musical talents like her mother and her grandmother. Aunt Natalie's singing career included broadcasts for the "Voice of America," appearances before numerous religious, fraternal and civic organizations and performances in the Philadelphia Convention Hall. Her repertoire was quite lengthy and included English, Italian, French, and German songs; operatic arias, Broadway show tunes, Negro spirituals, and Hebrew and Israeli music. She is probably one of the few members from the Dubois clan from Connecticut who had ever met and been in the presence of W. E. B. Du Bois. She writes that when she was a preteen she had met him at one of his events in New Haven at First Methodist Church, and she had the opportunity to speak with him.

Grandma Ro like Alexander Dubois, who would have been related to her by marriage, came from Northern families who had some type of slavery in their distant past. They themselves were years away from slavery and void of this type of service. They were free people of color. Second great-grandfather Alexander may have been closer to these things, but may not have experienced slavery himself in the Bahamas since his mother died when he was young. Since his father was a French physician, third great-grandfather Alexander more than likely had not himself experienced slavery. Grandma Ro knew nothing about slavery and servitude firsthand and did not even talk about it, if she in fact knew about it. Her parents were not former slaves and neither were her parent's parents.

The gradual emancipation of slaves had begun in 1834. Grandma was born more than fifty-five years later. But she had not mentioned Hempstead. Even my aunt knew of no conversations about Hempstead, New York, where our ancestors could have possibly been enslaved for a period of time. Aunt Natalie was shocked to learn of this since it appears that the Jackson seed originated in New Haven in the late sixteententh or early seventeenth century when Long Island was being disputed as a territory of Connecticut. In the end, New York was ruled as the state in which Long Island rested.

Churches and Organizations in the African American Community

The church was a major force for socialization and assimilation for the African American community. Several churches sprung up and prospered. Right down the street from where my grandmother lived was Daddy Grace's Church where I had performed as a dancer once as our dance group traveled from Waterbury to New Haven to participate in a youth event. The church was called the United House of Prayer for All People, and Sweet Daddy Grace was the leader. It was situated in the black section of Dixwell Avenue in New Haven around the corner from Henry Street and practically next door to my Grandma Ro's house. I remember clearly that the church building was pristine and perfectly white. It had a gigantic red, white, and blue banner on top that stated "Welcome All People."

Though New Haven was not his home or the location of his main parish, I am told Daddy Grace visited this place at least once a year. When he did, there was a great celebration on the streets in this African American neighborhood. Sweet Daddy Grace was the bishop who founded this church, and he was extravagantly flamboyant. He was born in the Cape Verde

Islands and was said to have owned one of the largest fleets of Cadillacs. He also had his own line of soaps and healing medicines. He performed miracles and baptisms, and he referred to himself as "the Boyfriend of the World."[33]

My family members were not of this denomination and as far as I know had not been members of or even attended his church. The United House of Prayer for All People was based on an apostolic doctrine and its common and shortened name was derived from Isaiah 56:7 where God says, "Mine house shall be called a house of prayer for all people."[34] My family members were Episcopalians, Baptists, Methodists, and Congregationalists.

Other social groups that were a part of my family's stability and growth were the masons, Grand Prince Hall Lodge of Masons, and the Elks. These social groups were established for survival purposes and for unity among the African American community. African Americans had to unite in some fashion if they wanted to survive. You had to be invited to be a member. Membership in these fraternal orders and their associated women's auxiliaries provided social activities for members, and, of great importance, membership provided standing within the African American community. In addition, these organizations set up both insurance and burial benefits for their members. These types of groups were of grave necessity to the African American community as African Americans continued to be prohibited from participating in the general population and were barred from such social organizations as the YMCA.

African Americans in New Haven were eventually given their own Y, which did not have the same quality or types of facilities such as a pool and a gymnasium. In spite of this, African Americans were prohibited from using the white facilities. Now I understand much better why my ancestors and parents were so heavily involved in their churches and organizations and why they actually held some of the highest positions in the fraternal orders. They were determined to make life better for the African American and particularly for their children. I know this firsthand and it started with them.

Among other things, my father held positions as Grand Master of the Prince Hall Grand Lodge for the State of Connecticut, Inc. and Grand Worthy Patron for the Prince Hall Grand Chapter, Order of Eastern Stars, State of Connecticut, Inc. earning him the title of Most Worshipful Past Grand Master of the Prince Hall Masonic Lodge. My grandfather was very active in both the Masons and the Elks and so were my great-grandparents Henry and Nettie Hatcher and my second great-granduncle Joseph Hatcher whose footsteps my father followed and who in previous years held the same Most Worshipful title as my dad. More properly stated my father held the same high position as his great-uncle. His great-uncle Joe, who lived up the street from us, is the one who led my father in this endeavor. Uncle Joe's son Edward was also very involved in the organization as were many of my relatives, past and present.

The Grand Lodge Prince Hall Masons of Connecticut purchased the Goffe Street School in May 1929. This is the same school that before it closed in 1874 had been strictly for the education of African American children and was the last segregated school to close. The Grand Lodge Prince Hall is still the State Headquarters for the Connecticut Prince Hall Grand Lodge of Connecticut and for the women's auxiliary, the Eastern Stars. The hall is located in New Haven on the corners of Goffe and Sperry Streets. My mother was very active in the Eastern Stars and holds the respected title of Past Grand Worthy Matron, as well as other illustrious titles, and was the first Worthy Matron for the Eastern Star in Waterbury, Connecticut, when they brought the Kellogg Lodge Temple on Bishop Street. In addition to the Masons, my granddaddy, Theodore W. Hatcher Sr. was a member of the Elks. The women's auxiliary for the Elks is called the Daughters and some of my ancestors were members of this organization as well. Great-uncle Alexander Jackson held high rank in the Elks as he served as Exultant Ruler, East Rock Lodge no. 141, in New Haven, Connecticut.

New Haven's Integrated School System and Job Opportunities

Following the civil war, the education of the African American was integrated into the white educational system, and in 1930, there were thirty-three African American students from New Haven in colleges.[35] The number was small, but so was the general population. In addition to education, job opportunities changed drastically with the industrialization and mechanization of jobs. Clerical workers, service, and salespeople were on a rise. In about 1915, my grandmother worked for Yale and then for a law firm and finally as a legal secretary for a judge. Historical data simply refers to Grandma's employer as Judge Celotto. My grandfather worked first as a clerk for a manufacturing company and then as a clerk at the US Post Office. Progress had already begun to occur for the African American.

On a whole, African Americans were excluded in the early to mid-1900s from working for private industry that included utility companies. African Americans had to depend on their community businesses for employment—for example, barber shops, restaurants, funeral parlors, and beauty shops. If other African Americans did not have jobs to pay for these services, then you know these businesses did not prosper to the extent needed. An extensive review of city directories indicates that during this era this section of town was populated primarily with artisans and craftsmen that included masons and blacksmiths. The carriage manufacturing industry was burgeoning as well.

In the earlier days, African American females often worked from home. They had extraordinary skills and were proficient in such tasks as baking, sewing, and laundering. But over time these things became more commercialized placing an additional strain on the African American families who had to depend on employment in commercialized laundries and in the garment factories while the wives and mothers had to take care of the family and raise their children. Likewise, the mothers had to ensure that their children made it safely to and from school. Finding employment was quite difficult for the African American men. They were excluded from working at industries that processed and manufactured rubber, cigar and tobacco, iron, and steel. But they were welcome to take the more difficult jobs such as drilling and digging inside tunnels, tending coke ovens, or carrying heavy loads.[36] No one else wanted these jobs. They also were most fitting as butchers or drivers for trucking firms or pressers in dry cleaning establishments. Some of my ancestors did these things. For example, my great-aunt Virginia who lived in Waterbury was a presser in the early 1900s and the husband to my great-grandaunt Charlotte was an express driver in Meriden, which is close to Waterbury, and a cousin in New York worked in the garment factories.

During the 1930s, most African Americans in the North continued to be employed as common laborers or in personal or domestic service. Other ethnic groups who immigrated to the United States, particularly Italians, began to take many of the jobs that were available to African Americans, and they locked the African American out of the hiring process by giving preference to their own people. Yet some of my ancestors managed to get past these roadblocks. In 1874, second great-grandfather William Jackson, was appointed by the governor as messenger in the Court of Common Pleas.[37] Second great-grandfather William is listed between 1863 and 1865 as colored. He worked as a school janitor, probably at

Yale since he is recognized by the African American Graduates of Yale, and then later worked as a messenger. The messenger job was a governor's appointment in the Court of Common Pleas. He lived on 9 Gilbert Street in New Haven in the Hill area southwest of the N. Frontage Road. I had heard something similar to this in the past, and I am honored that he received this distinguished appointment. Aunt Natalie advised me that great-uncle Alex spoke of this honor frequently.

Second great-grandfather, William H. Jackson, was born in Hempstead, New York, and moved to New Haven in the 1860s. He was married to my second great-grandmother Henrietta Jackson who was born in Hempstead as well. They both were born in 1836. They had three children: Henrietta Jackson (b. 1860), Benjamin W. Jackson (b. 1861), and Robert H. Jackson, my great-grandfather (b. 1863). The children were all born in New Haven, Connecticut.

Second great-grandmother Henrietta died at the young age of twenty-nine on October 10, 1865, in New Haven. Second great-grandfather William eventually married Charlotte Howard, a mulatto born in Hempstead, New York. Charlotte was living in the household of my second great-grandfather William with at least one of his children after my second great-grandmother died and probably was their housekeeper before then. She was listed as housekeeper until she and second great-grandfather married.

The African American struggle was unrelenting. The inferior civil status of African Americans continued through the 1860s and 1870s. African Americans continued to be victims of discrimination and bore the brunt of racist stereotypes and ridicule and so did the Italians who displaced African Americans from their menial jobs. But African Americans continued to try to survive through their memberships in separate and poorly funded churches, social clubs and self help groups. We still see these same things today. Yet the same suffering and the same pain was felt by at least two ethnicities, the African Americans and the Italians. Basically, Italians were also viewed as minorities.

In my opinion, even today, Italians identify themselves separately from the overall mainstream and like us felt the wrath of discrimination. But they were afforded the opportunity to establish their own vanguard, which resulted in them controlling certain aspects of this country and the employment of African Americans particularly in the State of Connecticut. I applaud their advancements as a minority group, but wish we did not have a target on our backs for disrespect and abuse by even them. But in spite of it all, so many African Americans have advanced to higher grounds and we are enjoying the fruits of our hard labor. The best example is the Honorable Barak Obama, the current president of the United States of America, and many others.

Spiritual Living

Churches continue to be some of the most segregated institutions today, and their inspirational messages lean toward the needs and membership of the congregation. Jesus is portrayed by both black and white as a white man with blue eyes and blonde wavy hair. But the Bible addresses neither the race nor physical appearance of Jesus in a direct and descriptive manner before his death. I question the whiteness of his skin, his blue eyes, and wavy hair. If he appeared that way, how could he have hidden himself in Egypt? He would have stood out like a sore thumb. Next, he was born and raised in the Middle East where people were people of color. But I will not argue this point because God loves all his children and we are his creation. He created every hair on our heads. In Matthew 10:30, Jesus speaks these words: "But the very hairs of your head are all numbered." I personally will not accept Jesus as a white man—but each man is entitled to hold his own opinion about this. Nevertheless, until we see him again, we may not know or agree on Jesus's physical appearance. Just to know him is enough for me. Even the scholars cannot agree, and there are various impressions of Jesus ranging from a white Aryan Jesus to a black African Jesus.[38] I do know he was a descendant of the Jews.

I visited white churches on occasion as they spent time apologizing for their parishioners not being happy with people of color joining them in worship. So I know to an extent what it may have felt like in those earlier days. I asked myself why I wanted to be a part of such a service. It was not right. If they didn't want me to worship with them, then they couldn't do anything to help me prosper and receive the blessings promised to me by the Lord. But I do know that as long as any preacher sticks to the Word contained in the Bible, I am inspired, and I will praise God anyway in the good and the bad times. We have to know and respect what the Bible says. It's not about us anyway. It is about God. We must know that God is no respecter of persons. In fact, Acts 10:24 conveys the message through Peter that God shows no partiality toward his people. Anyone who fears him and does what is right is acceptable to Him. So my ancestors just wanted to experience this pleasure afforded by God and founded their own churches.

These comments are not meant to be a slight toward anyone's church or to diminish other people's form of worship. They merely express my feelings and my preference for my worship and praise to God. I don't want to have to apologize for my color. I just want to praise God for allowing me to be one of his children. I just need to comfortably glorify God in the fashion in which he made me. I need a true spiritual experience and an overwhelming excitement for the Lord out of respect for God's mercy and his grace toward me and my people. Truthfully, if it had not been for the Lord on my side, I have no idea where I would be today. That deserves a big Amen and a hand clap of praise.

As I recall, New Haven continues to be a place where African American poverty is at issue. It has been a while since I have spent time there, but one of my cousins informed me of this continuing dilemma. Just look at some of the deprived communities. Self-hatred is at the forefront of our African American youth across this country and in big cities as they direct their attention to killing and destroying their own people. One of the top Ivy League schools, Yale University, is located not far from this nonsense. A war among one's own people is quite evident.

But we fought in the civil war and wars to follow. Even then African Americans were assigned to segregated units. Some of my ancestors, specifically, my second great-granduncles Colonel John Dubois and Private/Undercook Alfred Dubois, and my father, Warrant Officer Theodore W. Hatcher Jr. served at different times, but prejudice was still widespread and occurred equally in the military. Colored units were where colored people served. United States Colored Troops fought with the Union for their own freedom, but experienced few or none of the same privileges. Specifically, one of my great-granduncles listed above, Colonel John D. Dubois served during the civil war and died of consumption on September 17, 1861. His brother Alfred, father to WEB, enlisted December 8, 1864, and his residence was listed as Madison, Connecticut. Madison is a town in the southeastern corner of New Haven County, Connecticut, occupying a central location on Connecticut's Long Island Sound shoreline and was similar to another town where he was known to have lived and that was Milford, Connecticut. My father enlisted in the US Army on May 25, 1942, with his residence listed as Connecticut, also in New Haven County. He serviced in World War II as a warrant officer.

Some years ago, my oldest sister, Lt. Colonel Barbara J. Hatcher, served as chief nurse for both the 115th Combat Support Hospital (CSH) and the Mobile Army Surgical Hospital (MASH) when her unit was mobilized. Once in Saudi Arabia, during Operation Desert Shield/Desert Storm, her unit was combined with an active duty unit from Germany, and this expanded CSH was the farthest forward medical entity in the war zone where she served as assistant chief nurse. She is a veteran of a foreign war. Our cousin, Harold Garner Jr., was there at the same time though they did not come into contact with each other. The pain of war will forever linger.

As African Americans left and some escaped Hempstead, New York, they settled in such places as New Haven and Bridgeport, Connecticut. Many had mixed with the Indians on Long Island. They were less obviously of Indian extract and looked more like their African ancestry as many were listed in the census as black. I looked up those who were known to be part Shinnecock Indian with the surname Cuffee and who are related to me on the Jackson side, and they too were listed as black. Some moved to Bridgeport and continued to be listed in the same manner. I know for a fact that God had adorned them with strong African American characteristics accordingly. Then there have been some discussions about our family connections to Paul Cuffee from Massachusetts whose paternal African roots were from Sierra Leone and his mother was an Indian. He belonged to a tribe, the Wampanoag, which closely resembled the Shinnecock. He was a shipper who pirated freed and enslaved blacks back to Africa. Also, my cousin Katherine states that her mother's father was of American Indian ancestry, but she does not recall any Indian ancestry on the Jackson side. She was quite familiar with the Madagascan heritage on the Jackson side.

My third great-grandfather Alexander Dubois worked on the New Haven–New York boats. He himself was born in the Bahamas to a white Frenchman who was a physician, Dr. James Dubois, and one of his slave mistresses who remains unknown. But when third great-grandfather Alexander was brought to America after the supposed death of his mother, he lived as a "free person of color" throughout his duration in America. He was brought to America along with his brother John, and they attended gentleman's school in Chesire until their father passed. Third great-grandfather Alexander had to have been not much older than eight and his white family in New York clearly identified his brother and him as black. I don't know what happened to third great-grandfather Alexander between the death of his father and his coming-of-age. I do know for years he lived in New Haven and was very active in civil rights. Besides St. Luke's Episcopal Church in New Haven, he was also connected to a private Episcopal school in Cheshire, New Haven County, Connecticut. He is best known today as the grandfather to W. E. B. Du Bois. According to WEB's writings, it appears that he and his grandfather had only met once though they may have written to each other from time to time.

In spite of this single meeting, WEB seemed to have been somewhat familiar with his grandfather's movements to and from the islands and his activity with St. Luke's Episcopal Church in New Haven. He may have read excerpts from his grandfather's diary. Unlike third great-grandfather's son Alfred's relationship with WEB, third great-grandfather Alexander raised his children by his wife, Sarah Marsh Lewis, and his second wife, Mary Emily Jacklyn, whom he married sometime after third great-grandmother Sarah's death in 1834. They too had children.

My second great-grandfather Henry was one of the older sons and most likely the oldest born to third great-grandparents Alexander and Sarah. He was definitely older than the children born to the second wife and older than his half-brother Alfred who was WEB's father. According to WEB, his grandfather Alexander had several children with Sarah Marsh Lewis.[39] I tried to identify the others born to my third great-grandparents Alexander and Sarah, and I am not sure if I am totally correct. Their children had to have been born between 1824 since my third great-grandparents married on the 4 May 1823 and prior to my third great-grandmother's death in 1834. I am more than sure that second great-grandfather Henry, their oldest son, had other relatives born and raised in New Haven and New York. And the following is my belief. We are who we are because of those who came before us. Our progenitors hold great significance in our lives. And a spiritual life is a part of successful living.

In New Haven, Connecticut, Episcopal churches and African congregations were on the rise. It took almost twenty years from the start of this process before St. Luke's Episcopal Church was established. Prior to the establishment of these churches, African Americans were forced to the rear balcony of the white churches, and I imagine they sat crowded on a few pews. I don't know about you, but I refuse to sit on a crowded pew in the gallery of the church because someone says so especially if it is based on my color. If those are the rules, I can and desire to praise the Lord without them. I am sure this is the same way our people felt during the earlier days. And they prayed and they prayed and they prayed.

We do not serve a God of confusion. In fact, in 1 Corinthians 14:33, it is clearly stated that "God is not the author of confusion, but of peace, as in all churches of the saints." My conclusion is that you must have the devil in you to abuse and mistreat others. I know if I had to depend on these abusers for my only place of worship, I would use the power of God to pray the devil out of them right there in his church. Thank God for those who have the spirit of the Lord no matter what shape, size and no matter what color. Those who are truly anointed will ensure that the righteous survive. But I, like my ancestors, rather go my separate way. It is not about them or about me or us anyway. It is all about God. So efforts were under way to establish African American churches. Simultaneously, the white churches were undertaking efforts to establish missionaries in Sierra Leone to expand their control.

Third great-grandfather Alexander Dubois was deeply involved in this religious movement involving free worship for African Americans and, therefore, supported separate churches. He obviously was aware of the scripture contained in 1 Peter 3:9-12 in which God says, "Not rendering evil for evil, or railing for railing, but contrariwise blessings; knowing that ye are thereunto called, that ye shall inherit a blessing." It goes on to say that "for he that will love life, and see good days, let him refrain his tongue from evil, and his lips that they speak no guile; Let him eschew evil, and do good, let him seek peace and ensue it. For the eyes of the Lord are over the righteous, and his ears are open unto their prayers; but the face of the Lord is against them that do evil." The results of this religious movement and the establishment of St. Luke's Episcopal Church did not come to fruition until ten years after third great-grandmother Sarah Marsh Lewis had passed in 1834 at the age of thirty in New Haven. No one I knew personally had yet been born. The oldest member of my ancestors whose last name was Dubois in whose presence I would have been as a child would have been my great-grandmother Nettie who was born in 1871 in Cheshire, Connecticut, and died in 1951 in Waterbury, Connecticut.

I don't know for how long, but African American members of the white Trinity Church met to organize St. Luke's Church. They were literally tired of being restricted to the back of the church. They were allowed to sit only in the gallery, which we now call the balcony of the church. Records indicate there were forty-six African American members at that time who were a combination of slaves, freed people and free people of color.[40] They were spiritually ignored and ridiculed in the presence of the Lord. So they instead opted for their own separate churches as a way to comfortably praise the Lord because God is worthy of the highest praise free of worldly nonsense. The Lord is going to fix this. W. E. B Du Bois himself writes about his grandfather Alexander's revolt to separate because of the clearness that black folks were not welcome by white Episcopalians of the Trinity Parish in New Haven.[41]

Though most books, including those written by WEB himself, state WEB had little contact with his grandfather, he obviously must have kept in touch to an extent or read excerpts from his diary and learned of his frustrations and efforts toward obtaining equality and his demands for equal treatment. But from his writings and some of his assumptions it is obvious that he did not know his grandfather Alexander well.

Separate churches seemed to be a great compromise. It may have been these and subsequent frustrations that led third great-grandfather Alexander to move from Connecticut to Massachusetts. Just help us build this church and ordain our people with the authority already given by God. Enough was enough and Alexander and his partners were outraged and were forced to build their own house of worship. They did so with so much dignity and so much faithfulness that these churches still stand today. Psalm 68:19 states "Blessed be the Lord, who daily loadeth us with benefits, even the God of our salvation. Sé-lah." Joshua 24:15 says, "But as for me and my house, we will serve the Lord."

But in spite of his accomplishments in New Haven, third great-grandfather Alexander moved to Springfield, Hamden, Massachusetts and was listed as a steward and throughout his time in this country he was a free person of color. He was living with his wife, the former Mary Emily Jacklyn, and two of their young children: Henrietta, born about 1836 and John, born about 1844. Their third child, Charlotte had not yet been born. Henrietta appears to have been born in New Haven and John in Springfield, Massachusetts and probably Charlotte as well.

During the 1850 census, third great-grandfather Alexander is living in close proximity to a Benjamin Young who is listed as a mulatto barber from Washington DC who is married to Louisa from New York. Third great-grandfather Alexander is also listed as a mulatto. Others around him were listed as white. Many of the white people had immigrated to America and worked as teamsters, clergymen, clerks, joiners who were a type of carpenter, millworkers, machinists, blacksmiths, and I even located a tin man.

In 1860, third great-grandfather Alexander and his second family are located in Agawam, Massachusetts, where he purchased real estate and was listed as a farmer. Their grown daughter, Henrietta, was still living with them. He is the only mulatto listed in this vicinity while the rest of the farmers, merchants and wool manufacturers, to name a few, are listed as white. He owns $4,000 in real estate and $455 in other assets. The value of the real estate of the whites who lived around him was much less. Third great-grandfather Alexander was the wealthiest of them all as indicated on that particular census page.

Agawam sits on the western side of the Connecticut River directly across from Springfield, Massachusetts. The Indian village originally sited on the west bank was known as Agawam and so were the local Indians called the same. Fish were unloaded here from canoes for curing on the flats at the mouth of the Westfield River. Agawam furnished 172 men who fought in the American civil war, twenty-two of whom died in battle or of disease.[42] As stated previously, two of third great-grandfather's children served in this war and one lived in this area and the other in Madison, Connecticut, when they enlisted in the military. They were definitely living in this Massachusetts area at one point and around this time. Second great-granduncle John became a member of the colored troops and was promoted to the ranks of colonel. He died from consumption on September 17, 1861, at the young age of nineteen. His half-brother, second great-granduncle Alfred, father to WEB, was also a member of the colored troops. He enlisted on December 8, 1864, and he showed his residence as Madison, Connecticut. He deserted from the military in 1865 but he returned to make things right. He was a private and then he advanced to an undercook.

In 1860, the population of Agawam was 1,698 people and it still remains a small town with 28,438 residents. Agawam definitely increased in population from the time it was originally developed. I imagine third great-grandfather Alexander wanted to escape the city after his accomplishments in New Haven, and he wanted to rest in unsettled land where he could find peace in the hills and by the water. Also, he could participate as a forerunner and earn a more than decent income in this part of the country that was under development and produced crops.

In the 1900s, Agawam was known for its distillery. Cotton and wool mills were also erected. Tobacco was one of the important crops grown in these colonial times. In addition, cranberries, corn, pumpkins, squash, and other vegetables and rice were among the products of the state. Massachusetts overall was a farming and seafaring colony and is now a leader in the manufacture of high-technology products. Being a farmer and a grocer, it probably served third great-grandfather financially well to move to Agawam, Massachusetts, with his second wife, Mary Emily Jacklyn Dubois, and their children. In 1873, he was living with his third wife, Annie M. Dubois, in New Bedford, Bristol, Massachusetts, at 93 Acushnet Avenue. His second wife, Mary Emily, had passed prior to his third marriage to Annie M. Dubois. It is in New Bedford, Bristol, Massachusetts, where third great-grandfather Alexander passed on 9 December 1887.

The Movement Toward Freedom in
New Haven, Connecticut

Reverend Harry Croswell was a key figure in assisting the African American in this spiritual effort toward freedom.[43] He was known to visit his black parishioners in their homes in New Haven and actually visited third great-grandfather Alexander's home at that time and the home of other organizers as the organization of St. Luke's Church was under way.[44] In 1844, in either late April or early May, St. Luke's was formerly admitted as a parish in the diocese of Connecticut. No wonder the Gospel of Luke has always been my favorite book out of the four gospels. Original officers were Peter Vogelsang, clerk; Alexander Dubois, treasurer; Henry S. Merriman, warden; and Richard Green, vestryman, a longtime resident of New Haven.[45]

St. Luke's was called to establish a Haitian mission field and to expand the Episcopalian Church to Haiti. Their focus was emigration to this beautiful land of Haiti with its green trees and blue waters and pretty consistent climate. A lot of slum districts exist in Haiti today and French is their main language though the people are mainly from African descent. Haiti is where third great-grandfather's son Alfred was born to a Haitian woman in 1835 in what was then Santo Domingo. The birth of third great-grandfather Alexander's son Alfred occurred some years before the St. Luke mission.

A colony in Drouillard, which is on the outskirts of Port-au-Prince, Haiti, was established as part of this mission. This Drouillard section of Port-au-Prince is the same place victimized by the devastating earthquake of 2010. An article written about or by Doctors without Borders indicates that "nearly everyone in the country lost a relative, friend, or neighbor in the earthquake that hit that day." Others are still recovering both physically and psychologically, wounds so deep that they are hard to heal. This Caribbean city is still crumbled and in ruins and has yet to recover from this devastating and catastrophic event.[46]

Currently, the slum districts are listed as a place that no one should visit at this time. In addition to Port-au-Prince, other slum districts damaged from this disaster include Carrefour, Cité Soliel, Martissant, and Bel Air. Bel Air is the first "quartier" of Port-au-France a place where the upper class once lived but is now a part of the poor area.[47] In 1835, St. Luke's Episcopal Church was interested in Haiti as part of its mission. St. Luke's is listed as the third oldest African American church in the United States and one of the most beautiful African American churches in this country. The Jackson family belonged to this church and so too their children and their children's children.

We must always remember that our only purpose here on earth is to serve and please the Almighty God, our Lord and our Savior. It is about recognizing that we are blessed and enlightened by the rich wisdom of Jehovah God through his Son and the Holy Spirit. Once we recognize Jesus, knowledge is attainable and the sky is the only limit. And if we are really blessed and anointed by the Spirit of the Lord, we can rise above the sky and we can touch God and the hem of Jesus's garment by way of the Holy Spirit. God has given us wings like eagles so we might as well fly. We might as well soar.

I am proud to say that third great-grandfather Alexander Dubois was a part of this earlier mission, and I wish I could do something about the pain and suffering that recently occurred in Haiti. In summary, third great-grandfather Alexander was born in 1803 to a white doctor and his slave mistress in Long Bay, Bahamas, which is not far from Haiti. He married his wife, my third great-grandmother, the former Sarah Marsh Lewis, on 4 May 1823. She was probably born in New Haven in 1804 and died there on 9 July 1834 at the age of thirty. Third great-grandfather Alexander died in New Bedford, Massachusetts, on 9 December 1887.

The mother to third great-grandfather Alexander's son Alfred, father to W. E. B Dubois who was one of my second great-granduncles, was an unknown Haitian woman, and she birthed Alfred in 1835 in Santo Domingo. I find no evidence that WEB's paternal grandmother, Alfred's mother, was ever married to my third great-grandfather Alexander.

Second great-granduncle Alfred married Mary F. Silvina Burghardt on 3 February 1867 and left her and their son WEB shortly thereafter when WEB was two or three years old. According to WEB, when he left them they never heard from him again. We do know by census records that after leaving his family, second great-granduncle Alfred at some point lived in Milford, Connecticut, where he was employed as a barber. In his earlier years, he lived with his father and his father's second wife, Mary, and their children, his half siblings, in Massachusetts. At some point and before his marriage, he joined the military during the civil war as a member of the Colored troops.

New York Ancestry

Hempstead, Long Island, New York

Not far across the water between the coast of Connecticut and the easterly most coast of New York, you can see the shores of Long Island, New York. My aunt Natalie was an avid swimmer, and I am told that she used to swim in these waters off the shore of New Haven when she was a young teen. When I was a young person, my family and I ate on these shores. Most of us preferred to eat at Jimmie's Seafood Restaurant, but Grandma Ro preferred Turk's. We still go there today to eat at Jimmie's. We would go to the amusement park in West Haven called Savin Rock when I was a youngster, and I would often gaze at the Long Island shore that was a little distance from where we were. It was so peaceful. We spent a lot of time with the Judge family, my father's foster siblings, on Long Island, mainly

Jamaica, Queens, Long Island. Every now and then we would go to the New York and New Haven beaches or to the amusement parks. But it was spending quality time with family that was of utmost importance in both places. From time to time, relatives from New York would meet us at Savin Rock for a family outing. The one ride that I would not go on at Savin Rick was that rickety roller coaster that was suspended out into the Long Island Sound. I believe it was called the Thunderbolt. It was located on a pier and consisted of a mile-long track. Its straining sound was frightening and echoed danger to me. So I never went on that ride.

This area of New Haven was known as West Haven, and it is located on the New Haven Harbor on the northern shore of Long Island Sound in New Haven County. It comprises a part of the New York-Newark-Bridgeport, New York-New Jersey-Connecticut-Pennsylvania Combined Statistical Area.[48] Some of my Jackson ancestors lived in West Haven at one time. But never did I imagine that some of our ancient ancestors were born on Long Island. They may have arrived on this island in or around 1664, or they moved from New Haven to Long Island in the 1700s. No matter what, my fourth great-grandparents lived and may have even been born in New York and their children to include my third great-grandparents were definitely born in Hempstead in the 1780s. Their children and some grandchildren were born in Hempstead as well.

But something was brewing across these waters during the eighteenth century. A ferry line was established to take passengers back and forth between Connecticut and New York. Several wealthy men from Connecticut seized the opportunity to purchase undeveloped land on this island for close to nothing as the Native Indians thought it prosperous to sell their land to the white man. But after selling the land, these same Indians were taken by these same white purchasers as slaves.

Tradition has it that our ancestors mingled with and married those who were full or part Indian and we could have tribal blood from many years ago. I am not sure, and it was so long ago that it doesn't really matter except for historical purposes. I have yet to find the actual evidence. But what I do know is that those with any amount of African blood living on Long Island were listed as black and looked pretty much accordingly, even when mixed. The African bloodline was strong and Africans had the most dominant genes and features, no matter with whom we mixed. But we do know for sure that mixing did occur especially since the African male slaves outnumbered the African female slaves on this island. Since there were only a few families in Hempstead at the time, I assume fewer African or Indian women were needed to tend to the house chores and to care for the few children.

Because slavery on Long Island was abolished many years before our more recent ancestors were born, no discussion ever occurred between family members about this aspect of our ancestry. If Dad were alive today, I have a strong feeling that he would have been amazed, or maybe he already knew these things. It is hard to say. I do not recall my Grandma Ro discussing this factor, and as I recall, she did not mention that some of our ancestors were born in Hempstead, Long Island, New York. But my cousin Katherine Jackson Harris, first cousin to me and my father and niece to my grandmother, was somewhat aware and was even more aware that the Jackson seed landed in America in the late sixteenth or early seventeenth century and the Jackson seed probably landed first in the New Haven area.

Long Island is located not far off the shores of New Haven. I spent my teenage years in Queens and Hempstead, and I always felt more like a New Yorker, which was unbeknownst to me a strong part of my ancient heritage, and it felt like home. It was so familiar to me, and I actually wanted to move there when I became a teenager. If it had not been for my father's government job and his strong

Connecticut roots, I may have convinced Mom and Dad to move to New York. I had great dreams as a dancer. Also, Dad and Mom loved his foster brothers and sisters, the Judges, so much and we grew up as true family. He loved his sister, Aunt Natalie, equally as much and being blood probably more than one can imagine. Instead, I spent a lot of quality time on Long Island with my fictive cousin Brenda Judge Coleman, and I had both New York and Connecticut ways. I embraced them both. I was also close to Brenda's two siblings, Clayton and Jackie, and intermingled with and love dearly other members of the Judge family.

It took all these years for me to get an understanding why my soul and spirit was that of a New Yorker and why it felt like my home. People still recognize my New York spirit because I spent so much time there and my ancestors are buried there and are still resting in peace there. Just yesterday an African American restaurateur approached me and said, "You are a New Yorker." I always answer "Yes, a New Yorker born and raised in Connecticut who spent a lot of my time growing up in New York with extended family." New York was indeed my second home. Not only was he from New York but his family was from Haiti and like me he had French ancestry. He stated that his mother was of French descent and his father was Haitian. He felt I looked just like his sister. We exchanged a few French words and departed with "Au revoir, a bientot."

As stated earlier, most of the Judge children with whom my father was raised lived on Long Island. We would visit them quite often on the weekends where they had such good times together. I would hang out with my fictive cousin, Brenda Judge, and I loved dressing and acting like a New Yorker accordingly. I had good friends in both New York and Connecticut. I socialized quite a bit in New York, and New York was the place I loved the most. And now I know that some of my ancient ancestors were born and were buried where I truly felt at home. I have some fond memories of Long Island. I am still very close with my fictive cousin, Jackie Judge Jacobs, who is Brenda's sister, and she lives in Brooklyn, New York. We were raised as family.

Not only were the Jackson roots in New York, so were some of the Dubois roots. At least one ancient cousin, Josephine Ridley Allen, who was daughter to one of the Dubois sisters, the former Sarah Louise Dubois, had moved from Waterbury, Connecticut, to Manhattan, New York, with her children. After the death of her father in Waterbury, her mother, my great-grandaunt Sarah Louise Dubois Ridley, moved to Manhattan, and she lived with her daughter. A couple of my great-grandaunt's grandchildren were born there as well.

Sarah Louise Dubois Ridley was sister to my great-grandmother Nettie Dubois Hatcher whose husband was my great-grandfather Henry Hatcher. In 1907, my great-grandfather Henry had purchased outright the home on Bronson Street in Waterbury, Connecticut, a home I grew up in after our move from the Hill in Waterbury. Our family still owns this property. There was never a mortgage on this house. Praise God! Heaven knows what happened to second great-granduncle John, brother to third great-grandfather Alexander, who moved to New York from Cheshire as a young boy and it is rumored that he possibly passed as white. And then there were the white Dubois kin who lived and settled in Poughkeepsie, New York, and probably other places in New York. I am more than sure there are others whom I don't even know.

Who would have thought Hempstead, Nassau County, New York, or Flushing or Brooklyn would be the place where things were developing for the African American during these earlier years. This newfound information took me by surprise, though it made a lot of sense. Our grandmother always stated that we were free people of color and we were born in the North. Being free was factual for the majority of our family throughout the generations. She probably had no clue about Hempstead or simply didn't speak about it. But I think she would have told us. As I stated earlier, my aunt Natalie was also surprised about our ancient ancestors in Hempstead. She knew for sure that her mother was of Madagascan ancestry, but did not know that any of her ancestors were born and settled in Hempstead.

Grandma knew and was proud of her Madagascan ancestry, which was more than likely on her mother's side. She may not have known that her father's father and mother, William H. and Henrietta L. Jackson, were born in and moved from Hempstead to New Haven, probably by way of the New York-New Haven boats. This would be the same boats that third great-grandfather Alexander Dubois often worked on. And Grandma may not have known that her great-grandparents Semon and Leonora were born in Hempstead, Queens, New York, as well. She simply did not speak about New York even if she knew this.

But I am told by Uncle Alex's grandson, Chris Cuffey, who still lives in Hempstead that Grandma's brother, who is my grand-uncle Alexander, often visited some of the Jackson relatives there. Henry Francis Cuffey, Chris's father and a son to grand-uncle Alex, was born in Connecticut, I believe Bridgeport, and he said he too was not aware that Hempstead was where ancient members of the Jackson family were born. Uncle Alex did not speak about Hempstead to us nor to some of his other children that were born and raised in New Haven. It appears he may have spoken about this place to at least his older daughter Katherine who wasn't as surprised as the rest of us. But our bloodline appeared to have moved back and forth from Connecticut to New York. According to records and those with prior knowledge, the Jackson seed originated in New Haven in the late sixteenth or early seventeenth century.

Nevertheless, my grand-uncle Alex's family in New Haven and in New York did not intermingle and did not know much about each other. They were raised separately because of surrounding circumstances. His son, Henry Francis Cuffey, is my first cousin one time removed who lives in Hempstead, New York. His family was not known to us as family. But I knew Uncle Alex's grandson, Chris, as a friend. Occasionally, when visiting my cousin Brenda Judge, I shared time with him. He was a very good friend of my cousin's husband, Edward Coleman. Chris and I had no clue that we were blood family until many years later. It is really a small world. I had the pleasure recently to speak to my cousins Francis and Chris, and I obtained additional information from them, and I shared other information with them.

I don't think my second great-grandparents William and Henrietta had to escape Hempstead, New York, like I am told other Long Island natives did to avoid the continuous hard labor in such occupations as whaling. In the 1850 census, second great-grandfather William and his father and the rest of his family were listed as free inhabitants on Long Island before his move to New Haven when he was a young man. As I stated earlier, I searched records of some of those who were part Shinnecock and who moved to Connecticut during that time period, and they are clearly listed on the census as black. It seems on Long Island if one was of African descent, partial or whole, he or she was considered black.

The once large Indian population on Long Island had dwindled mainly due to deaths from diseases such as smallpox spread by the European colonists. The few who survived and were full-blooded Indian escaped to the west. The decline of the full-blooded Shinnecock Indians caused them to mix heavily with the Africans and to a lesser degree the whites on the island. Research contained in an article entitled, "the Shinnecock Nation" states that most Shinnecock look black but identify as Native American.[49] Therefore, as stated above, the Shinnecock Indians are well-known to be both biracial and others triracial, with ample African and white ancestry.[50]

Having said this, I am certain that at least one or both of third great-grandfather Semon's parents may have been relocated to Hempstead from somewhere in Africa or from the West Indies or from New Haven, and DNA tests reveal that he or his progenitors may have descended from Ghana, prior to 1787. It is therefore more probable than not that someone in this bloodline served as a slave on Long Island or in New Haven. This may or may not have included our third great-grandparents.

Third great-grandfather Semon's wife, my third great-grandmother Leonora Jackson, was born in Hempstead, Long Island, New York, just as he was. The 1870 census shows her birth about 1785 or possibly 1787, and she is living with one of her sons, Charles Jackson, who was forty-three along with two younger Jackson children, Salatheal, age seven and Druscilla Jackson age six. Charles had previously been listed with his father Semon. It appears that third great-grandfather Semon may have passed before 1870. Third great-grandmother Leonora is eighty-five years old at the time of the 1870 census. If third great-grandfather Semon had been alive in 1870, he would have been 85 as well. Because of some of our ancestor's longevity and that of other slaves or freed people in Hempstead, it is apparent that the holders ensured the African Americans on the island had good medical care and good nutrition.

Third great-grandmother Leonora's great-granddaughter, my Grandma Ro, carried her name as her middle name. Grandma Ro's full birth name was Romietta Leonora Jackson. Assigning a middle name of an ancestor was a tradition in our family. The middle name was often used as a tracer or as an honor and linked us to the past. My aunt Natalie's full name at birth was Natalie Roberta Hatcher. She just advised me that she was given her middle name after her grandfather, Robert Jackson. My father, Theodore William Hatcher Jr. and my grandfather, Theodore William Hatcher Sr. were assigned the middle name William after my grandfather's grandfather. I believe Granddaddy's sister Virginia may have carried the middle name Odrick as did her cousin Raymond who definitely carried that middle name. She is listed on the census as Virginia O. Hatcher.

In Hempstead's census, our Jackson family is listed as black. This is in line with others who may have been mixed-people or totally of African descent. Being mixed, particularly with European or even Indian blood, makes it a little difficult to know for sure the fullness of our ancestry to the point of certainty. Other than the African American seed, other seeds are pretty obscure. Again, there is no doubt that we were blessed with African ancestry—very strong genes.

Unlike his parents and his parent's parents, great-grandfather Robert H. Jackson was born in New Haven, Connecticut. I recently discovered that he may not have been the first generation born there. I am still surprised that there are some things that weren't discussed in the past for whatever reason. I strongly believe since our ancient ancestors on Hempstead were able to be traced back as living in Hempstead to the third great-grandparents and possibly even the fourth great-grandparents since our third great-grandparents were born there, they were most likely subjected to some sort of servitude and may have been freed in accordance to the law. Nevertheless, it doesn't matter if they were African, West Indian, or Indian. I suspect they were somehow subjected to serfdom many moons and many years ago.

There were approximately thirteen tribes on Long Island, and the population was very small and very few slaves in the beginning. Supposedly, male slaves greatly outnumbered the female slaves. It would make sense that some mixing occurred, but it may not be necessarily so for all families. As for the Jackson family, such information is vague at this time. I used to feel the native spirit when I was a child, but I truly lost that feeling when I left the Connecticut area. Anyway, the reality is that I have all along only completely felt what I am and how I look and that is African American and this is a sure thing.

This search is not to determine who I am, I already know. This search is about finding my ancestors and at the same gaining some sense of my racial ancestry. Even so, if we had mixed blood on Long Island, it was so long ago. But I do know without a doubt that my people were black, mixed or not, and came from across the waters on a most devastating and demeaning journey. Chained and brutalized. As far as the full-blooded Indian, diseases were rampant on Long Island and not many of the full-blooded Indians survived. Other conflicts with the colonists caused them to move further to the western part of America.

In summary, though Grandmother Ro knew and admired that we were free people of color, our original ancestors who arrived in America may have been subjected to some sort of servitude and even slavery. But the fact that the Jackson burial plot contains headstones back to the 1700s, I would wager a long period of freedom for the Jackson seed and so for the historical conception.

Third Great-Grandparents Semon and Leonora Jackson

Records show that second great-grandfather William H. Jackson lived with his family in Hempstead, New York, during the 1850 census as a free inhabitant, and he was born there in 1831. He lived with his father, third great-grandfather Semon Jackson, who was sixty-two years old at the time and who was born in Hempstead as well. Based on my research, it wasn't uncommon for a man and woman to father and give birth in their forties. It is much more unusual today. Also, living in the household are second great-grandfather William's brother, Charles, and probably his family. More information may have carried over to the next page of the census but is not available for view. It may be on that page that we would find our third great-grandmother or she may have been accounted for elsewhere. Chances are that my third great-grandparents Semon and Leonora had been born into slavery or servitude, and they themselves could have been slaves or servants or they may have been free. Since someone in their ancestry served as an assistant to one of the first black governors in New Haven, it is possible that they themselves may have been free. It must be noted however that black governors could also continue to be slaves. We do know their descendants, to include their children, were born free since slavery was ended on Long Island before their children were born.

I know the family's original name was not Jackson since our ancestors came on ships from across the waters, but I can probably piece together how third great-grandfather's parents may have chosen at least his first name that was uncommon. In studying the history of Hempstead, several Englishmen from Stamford, Connecticut, bought the Hempstead territory from the Indians in 1643. John Seamon and Robert Jackson were among them, and they purchased 1,500 acres of land from the Indians and settled upon it with their families.[51] They established quite a village and their family carried this wealth for many years living on Hempstead. New information however makes it obvious that the Jackson seed and surname may have started in New Haven, Connecticut, and the chosen name may or may not be related to these two men. However, these two families were not just wealthy in New York, they were wealthy in Connecticut as well and their status in Connecticut may have had some influence when the naming of African Americans occurred.

It is important to know that the first slaves who arrived on Hempstead directly from Africa arrived on August 6, 1655, from the West Indies and from Madagascar as well as from the West Coast of Africa. Again, it could be that third great-grandfather Semon's mother and father were slaves or servants for both or one of these two families mentioned above. It is even harder now to confirm this knowing that the Jackson seed and surname started in New Haven in the sixteenth or seventeenth century.

Not all slaves on Long Island were treated poorly, and my ancestors may have thought it proper to use at least the first name of one of these wealthy families in Hempstead when naming their son. On the other hand, it may be that these two things are not related at all. I have simply made an assumption regarding the origin of the name Semon.

The number of slaves that were owned by a man and his family was indicative of his wealth. Slaves were not of great numbers in Hempstead. In 1723, there were 1,123 slaves; in 1790, 2,039 slaves; and in 1810, only 800 slaves.[52] This same document reports that more men were held as slaves than women. The major public slave market for this area was on Wall Street and slaves sold at a high price: fifty pounds for a male, forty-five pounds for a female, and sixty pounds for a black woman and her child. The healthier the slave, the more valuable he or she was on the auction block. The slaves slept in the attics of smaller homes and had their own outbuildings when owned by the richer slave masters who had larger quarters. There were also white slaves in addition to those who were black or Indian, and there were white bond or indentured servants who served for five or six years before being freed. Some of the African slaves on Hempstead became restless and disenchanted and assembled themselves in a riotous manner. There was actually a major African American upheaval in 1741 that cost some lives.

However, at the point of the 1850 census, third great-grandfather Semon is listed as a black laborer, and he and his family are free. Still chances are that he may not have been free from the start. Many free and enslaved people of African ancestry were part of the development of Hempstead and other surrounding areas since 1655.

At the same time, Indians were also slaves, and as stated above, other Europeans were enslaved and indentured. As a side note, the Indians referred to the white man as pale faces. The white man referred to the Indian as hostile and rude. The Indians probably had a reason to be that way. After all, they had their land stolen from them for little or nothing and then the buyers enslaved them. That was cold.

Being mixed with black or Indian, or Madagascan and Ghanaian, or Jamaican and Antiguan didn't really matter. There were Africans, West Indians, and Indians who were serving as slaves, and as stated earlier, some Europeans were serving as slaves and bondservants. New York State and local laws freed the Indians from the institution of slavery prior to freeing the other slaves. Slavery in the state of New York was totally abolished in 1827, though most slaves had been freed by 1825.[53]

I truly loved Long Island and New York City even before I gained this ancestral knowledge. In my younger years, to include my teens and my early twenties and thirties, I truly felt a sense of home where my ancestors had lived, where they toiled and fought hard for their freedom. I would like to think they were free all along since we were told that we came from free people of color from the North. What I do know for sure is that at some point they were freed and the majority of our ancestors were forever free, but I am not convinced that they all were free on the shores of northern America in the very early years.

No matter what, those days were not pretty times, and I am sure there were a lot of private moments. If our ancestors could only talk! I do know their spirits are leading me in this quest. Those very moments were part of my fabric and created a tapestry that makes me who I am today. I so love them dearly as they overcame the odds and ensured that we were free. I embrace, applaud, and honor them. Based on information contained in various documents about slavery on Long Island, especially the document written by Anne Hartell, I have concluded and summarized my thoughts below regarding our ancestral journey in Hempstead.

Summary of Hempstead, Long Island, New York

Our Madagascan and West African ancestry existed in Hempstead, New York, during the time of slavery. Based on the birth dates of at least third great-grandparents Semon and Leonora Jackson who were born in New York, I would wager that they and/or their parents were subjected to slavery or servitude at one time. Also, Hempstead was not very heavily populated in those days making it easy to trace our ancestors to a certain point. Slavery was a big game in America and in other places. Some of the more powerful whites were landowners, and they engaged heavily in this institution. Slavery's sole purpose was wealth for them and them only. This wealth came at the expense of others and it took the slaves to finally demand an end to it. Those times in Hempstead and other places in New York were brutal for some while others seemed to survive, and they eventually found freedom. But even then they continued to serve as laborers as evidenced by third great-grandfather Semon who is listed in the 1850 census as a laborer. We have to remember that there wasn't much else to do during these developmental times. Things were being built and needed to be maintained and everyone needed to eat.

Some African Americans were victims of unwarranted brutality and untimely deaths. In defense, some of the African slaves would take the slaveholder's life and his belongings to ensure their freedom, and they would take off never to be seen again. The slaves on Long Island were not at all passive when it came to their freedom. After all, they were forced here under some extremely bad conditions. It seems as though Canada may have been one place and the key place for escape. Maybe this is where the Canuck connection occurred. Grandma Ro did at one point speak about French and/or Canadian ancestry when we went through the black power era. She said that we were ignoring our other ancestors from other foreign places. She just couldn't understand how we could purposely refer to ourselves as black. Being called Negro or colored was okay with her.

So some of the slaves escaped to Canada, and this may be where a number of black Canadians were born and raised. Nevertheless, within time, slaves on Long Island became intolerable to the white man and at the same time unprofitable in the scheme of things. So the white owners manumitted most of them. In actuality, the slaves, the Quakers, and others who opposed this institution helped put an end to it. Simultaneously, the economic reasons for slavery and serfdom had simply declined in the North.

Slavery was an unpleasant and inhumane institution anyway. And on Long Island, the slaves were freed before federal legislation mandated this. If they had not been freed at this time, it is obvious from the written stories that they would have freed themselves. The African American slaves in New York and especially on Long Island formed many upheavals and were very skilled and successful at escaping.

Based on the slaves' activities to regain their freedom, I conclude that overall the slaves on Long Island were not a docile people. Don't get me wrong. Some of those in the South were tough and rebelled as well—Nat Turner for one. And there were many others who were tough in the South as they made their escape from this wicked and vicious institution of slavery by differing means to include the Underground Railroad, runaway slaves, revolts, mutinies, and other similar attempts at gaining freedom. Some succeeded and others died. Some were able to endure, others were not. Through research and reenactments, it is clear that those of color were treated disgracefully and many were brought to their knees or hanged from a tree at an alarming rate. The difference between the North and the South was that the South had more support and a much greater need for this institution of slavery. It was profitable to the slave owner. Cheap labor was more than cheap. It was free. Even if the owners were required to feed them, they fed them their scraps, and they lived in substandard housing.

Profits were gained from the slaves working nonstop in the fields, chopping wood, hoeing and grinding corn and picking cotton, for starters. The women cooked, cleaned, and reared the children of their masters, they even breastfed them and served in other undeserving manners. Three meals were usually served during the 1800s and such tasks as cooking and cleaning dominated the female slaves' time. Cooking was originally done by digging an enclave in the ground, lighting a fire and then carrying pots on a long stick and placing the pot over the fire to cook and boil the food. Of course, the food had to be captured or farmed and spices had to be ground before the cooking task could even begin.

Within time, hearths were built in the log cabins making it a little more pleasant and allowed more time to be spent with the family. For the African American who was a slave or others who were indentured servants, these things were accomplished with no compensation while the white man in charge prospered beyond imagination. In the meantime, slaves were whipped and beaten and hanged and called out of their names on a constant basis.

It was more profitable to keep the slaves under control in the South by any means necessary. They did the work while the others rested and prospered. This was truly a demonized time when Satan unleashed those who served him to specifically brutalize God's people who were the slaves and the servants. These slave masters were just plain evil. There is no other explanation. The golden rule is that you either love God and your neighbors as yourself, or you love the world. Satan is the prince of the air, and he rules the world. There was definitely a spiritual battle going on. But these evil things only made my people turn to God and strengthen their faith in Him. They knew that it was God and God alone who deserved to be worshipped and praised in the good times and the bad times. They understood that the battle would eventually be won.

In the North, the profits just were not there. In fact, slavery was beginning to cost more than the profits being realized and so for the early dismantling of slavery in the North. On the other hand, some, particularly the Quakers, knew about righteousness and knew God's Word and probably did not want the wrath of God upon them. Besides holding people hostage just didn't feel right to a great number of the Northern whites. It was a game not to be played with or reckoned with if one had any Godly sense. The spiritual consequences were drastically eternal.

Unlike slaves in the South, Northern slaves lived in the white man's home either in attics or in separate quarters on the main grounds. Yet when slavery was in place, the consequence for fleeing and getting caught was the same brutal punishment in the North as it was in the South. It appears the opportunity of the Northern slaves to whip their master or other attackers back, if they could, was greater in the North. On Long Island, a lot of plotting for one's freedom went on and the white man knew it. Slaves would take off and never be seen again as they had the authority to sell themselves. Who in their right mind would sell themselves without planning a flight for freedom? You just can't keep a good, innocent and strong man down.

As early as 1644, the laws of New York recognized Indians as slaves, and the regulations concerning slaves generally applied to "Negro, Indian, Mulatto, and other slaves." Bond servants and slaves from European countries were definitely in the midst. Servitude and slavery were basically the same with slavery being designed for perpetuity and servitude for usually five to seven years. Indentured slaves were allowed to work toward their freedom. But it was all about wealth at the expense of others. The Indians remained slaves for many years and were freed by a 1778 New York law, about one hundred thirty-four years later.

Even today, many people are unaware of this history on Long Island and this includes those who now live there. I know I am simply shocked, but I can now say I am properly informed. I am more than convinced that the abolishment of slavery was at God's hand and some of those who were the holders in New York, and who were spiritual, actually felt and knew this type of cruel and unusual punishment to be a sin. We served our time and the Quakers and other abolitionists no longer wanted to take part. The supernatural took over, and they sensed they were wrong and probably without a doubt felt the wrath of God.

Slavery was finally abolished from the New York colony by a 1799 state law, requiring its gradual eradication. In 1827, almost 185 years ago, the state legislature passed a law prohibiting the holding of slaves in New York State all together though most had already been manumitted by 1825. The manumission of slaves on Long Island was about forty years or two generations before the Emancipation Proclamation.

It is my conclusion by way of the Spirit that some of my Northern ancestors served at some point as slaves or servants if only in the late sixteenth century or early seventeenth century when they inhabited Connecticut. I truly believe when first brought to this land, they had experienced a loss of their personal freedom particularly as people of color. On the other hand, they could have been free people of color for some strange reason. However, without proof, I cannot see how this was likely on Long Island. As we look at the full picture, we know that from the beginning the land in this country belonged to and had been inhabited by the Indians as they too unwillingly became slaves. As far as those born and raised in Hempstead, rich Europeans from Connecticut purchased this land from the Indians and purchased white, indentured slaves from other countries. They brought African slaves from East Africa, specifically, Madagascar, and from the West Indies and West Africa and other places where people of color originated or lived. Let it be known loud and clear. Slavery was a forced institution and had an economic purpose at the expense of our ancestors' freedom and their well-being.

And we shall never forget about the Indians who were at one time the only inhabitants in America. Also, since African men on Hempstead outnumbered the African female, intermarriage with the Indians was not a surprising affair. I know for sure that my ancient ancestors on my paternal grandmother's maternal side came from Madagascar at some point and now I have discovered that on the paternal side from West Africa, possibly from Ghana. Mixed or not, they were unmistakably black.

My grandmother loved her heritage as a Madagascan and talked about it quite frequently. Every time we were in her presence, and that was often, she would remind us of this. She really wanted us to embrace this. Based on Aunt Natalie's DNA, Grandma's mother was of Ethiopian and Madagascan ancestry, and she was reported to be one of the prettiest women in the world. She was a mulatto born in Washington DC and may have had non African ancestry as well. But Grandma didn't talk about that to the extent where I am able to remember such discussions. No matter what, we were definitely brought up to know that, without a shadow of a doubt, we are African Americans. I do not really think they cared in the least bit that we may have other ancestral blood. Unless they passed as white and therefore did not associate with us, no one in my family claimed themselves to be other than African American, and they carried themselves with great pride, self-assurance, and strength.

It must have been hard for any person of color to care about our European blood in those days. There was this misconception that we were products of the very people who hated us, who whipped and chained us, who stole us from our countries and enslaved us and called us out of our names. We now know differently. Most interracial children were born to indentured white woman and the African male. Fewer were fathered by the white man and the African female though this did exist as well. Grandma talked briefly about some other heritage when we began calling ourselves black. We knew something else was in the mix anyway. Unfortunately, we will always have a portion of our ancestry that we will never know. I respect those who are a part of our heritage, both the known and the unknown, in spite of it all.

The bottom line is that my sisters and I were the only grandchildren Grandma Ro had, and she wanted us to know about Madagascar. That must have been where her spirit rested and where she felt the most connected. Grandma Ro would invite my sister, Dr. Barbara J. Hatcher, for lunch while my sister was conducting her clinical study at Yale University as part of her college curriculum. Grandma Ro shared with her that she was in communication with a cousin who still lived in Madagascar. Grandma Ro and her Madagascan cousin would write each other, she said. Maybe one day I will find those letters.

Our Jackson Ancestors from New York and New Haven

ebrews 13:8 confirms that Jesus Christ is the same yesterday, today, and forever. Some of my ancestors on my maternal side of my father's mother were apparently brought to the United States from Madagascar, an island nation off the eastern coast of Africa. On the paternal side of his mother they may have come from West Africa and the West Indies and possibly Madagascar as well.

The section before this one gives you an idea of what was occurring on Long Island, New York. Those times were not at all simple. For such a small population, life was in fact complex. There was a lot going on not only on the farms but in the lives of those who were brought from other foreign places to include Madagascar, an island so remote from this country, and from places in West Africa and the West Indies. But the European settlers had run out of help and had already raped West Africa, so their pickings were getting slim. Also, the Indian population was small and many were unable to survive the European diseases and the Indians were dying at an unimaginable rate.

For some of our African ancestors who were Madagascan, the slave boats had previously traveled from East India, where East Indian slaves had already been brought to the south and intermingled with the African population. Strategically, they decided that for the North, they needed to focus on the West Indies and Madagascar. I strongly recommend that you read one of the most insightful documents regarding slavery on Long Islands: "Slavery on Long Island" by Anne Hartell, published 1943 in the Nassau County Historical Journal. I learned so much about some of our northern ancestors from this one document.

Hempstead, Long Island, New York (1850 Federal Census)

In 1850, the census became much more sophisticated than the prior enumerations. It contained specific instructions on what should be collected from its free inhabitants: the person's name; age as of the census day, which was June 1, 1850; sex; color; birthplace; the occupation of males over age fifteen; value of real estate; whether married within the previous year; whether deaf-mute, blind, insane, or "idiotic"; whether able to read or write for individuals over age twenty; and whether the person attended school within the previous year. No relationships were shown between members of a household in the 1850 census. The column to identify relationships to the head of the household was added in the 1870 census. The purpose of the census and its accuracy was for tax purposes and appropriation of seats in the House of Representatives.[54]

Some of our ancestors were included as early as the 1850 census, and therefore, they are easily located. Based on this, they were therefore free inhabitants as far back as 1850 and even before.

In addition to the previous pages, the following pages will focus on the Jackson side—the Madagascans, Ghanaians, and possibly West Indian people who lived in Hempstead, Long Island, New York, in the eighteenth and nineteenth centuries. Some ancestors and relatives are still living there today. Slavery in New York was costly to the European—approximately $5,000 in today's currency for each slave. Slaves were also brought in from British colonies in Barbados, Antigua, and Jamaica. The first Africans were brought to the southern part of North America around 1609 and to Long Island in 1665. Slaves were first indentured servants and then they were converted to slaves for life. At least the white man envisioned this as a lifelong thing. Some slaves served for life due to the timing of their deaths and others were freed for various reasons to include the manumission and emancipation of slaves. Again, God had a different plan in this battle between good and evil.

The Africans who came to Long Island originated from seven principals with Madagascar being one of them.[55] The majority of Africans came from the Western coast of Africa to include Nigeria, Congo, Angola, Ghana, Cameroon, and Senegal. Throughout my family's DNA are found the Madagascans, Ghanaians, and Senegalese, to name a few. Work on Long Island varied. Dairy and agricultural products were produced. Female slaves did kitchen work and prepared dairy products. Males were laborers who worked in the fields and did daily manor maintenance. Punishment for not completing one's task was rigorous.[56]

Long Island had bondservants from other places like England and Nova Scotia, and there is quite a bit of evidence that Africans, West Indians, and Indians were not the only ones enslaved in the New York colony. By 1807, African slave trade was outlawed in the

United States of America and the United Kingdom[57] though slavery remained.

Let us not forget these facts. Some of our ancestors were abused and were subjected to unsanitary and cruel and unusual treatment as they were brought involuntarily on slave ships. Many did not survive the travel from the continent of Africa and died en route. They were subjected to crammed and cramped conditions, they were chained, and they died from diseases such as dehydration, dysentery, and scurvy. Some ships sank and the slaves and everyone aboard drowned.

Then there were the mutinies by the slaves such as on the ship Meermin, a Dutch East India Company ship that transported Madagascans.[58] And let us not forget the Portuguese ship, Tecora, which transported the slaves who would later revolt aboard La Amistad at Mystic Seaport.[59] I am told that some of our ancestors were probably part of this revolt and were among those brought to court. We need to know these things. Some of our African ancestors were in the midst as they fought for their freedom. The Amistad case before the US Supreme Court, which is recorded as the first civil rights case in America, was decided in favor of the Africans, and they were returned to their homeland.[60] New Haven was home to the Amistad trial held in New Haven's United States District Court.

Second Great-Grandparents William and Henrietta Jackson

"I can do all things through Christ who strengtheneth me" (Philippians 4:13). The result of Aunt Natalie's DNA confirms some of what we already know. We are blessed with great-uncle Alexander's son, Dr. Bruce Jackson, who is Aunt Natalie's and my father's first cousin and my first cousin one time removed. Dr. Bruce is Head of the Biotechnology Programs at Massachusetts Bay Community College. Through this program, Bruce created the first and only forensic DNA program in the world. As such, this is the proper time to introduce him into this portion of the family. As I stated earlier, Aunt Natalie informed me recently that Bruce is an identical image of their grandfather, Robert Jackson. "When you see Bruce, you see him," she says. Bruce like other members of the Jackson family was a member of St. Luke's Episcopal Church in New Haven. It is so amazing when the story of one's ancestry unfolds. Each family born to one generation has eight great-grandparents with eight different stories to tell. This is one of them.

According to the expert Dr. Bruce Jackson, "our DNA fits the Ethiopian haplotype which is believed to be similar to Madagascar." He further states that "the world DNA databases (including our own) have led us to this conclusion." This explains my great-grandmother Henrietta's ancestry. Also, my great-grandfather Robert's father and mother were born in New York and West African ancestry is in the mix and is identified in Bruce's DNA. More information may be forthcoming.

My sister recalls Grandma Ro saying that our ancestors were free people. It definitely held true during the census of 1850 and it definitely held true for those who were born in Connecticut, New York, Massachusetts, Washington DC, Philadelphia, and other places in the North and some in the South were freed people, particularly in North Carolina. It appears that they were free people for a very long time though they may not have been forever free.

Recently my cousin Bruce Jackson advised me of some evidence of West African ancestry on the paternal side of the Jackson family. Based on his research and his travels throughout Africa, he suspects that the West African country from where some of our ancestors originated may have been Ghana. This West African seed more than likely originated in New Haven for Africans on the Jackson side who were transported to America.

I know about the slave trade in Ghana. I visited Ghana several years ago. When I first arrived in Ghana I felt as though I had arrived home. When I put that first foot down on African soil for the first time in my life, I was ecstatic and expressed thanks to God for this opportunity and for my safe arrival. But I have to admit that there is no place like the United States, and I was anxious to return home.

While in Ghana, I visited the Cape Coast castles where the slaves were held, and I learned quite a bit to include standing in "the Door of No Return." This was the exit used to board the Africans on the slave ships headed to various foreign lands. In addition to visiting these castles, one of the strangest experiences in Ghana, which totally caught me off guard was being regarded as just another foreigner by local Ghanaians and actually being referred to as "foreigner" or "white." I had been called a lot of names, but never "white." That was a first. I found out later that this was standard treatment of African Americans, and we were actually referred to as "obruni," the native term for whites in Ghana. I really didn't like this feeling and began to feel unfairly separated from my ancestry. In spite of it all, I enjoyed the experience immensely and learned and felt so much in my spirit. I could feel some of my ancestors as I roamed this African territory for the first time.

As far as the beginning of slavery in Ghana, captured Africans were held in the Cape Coast castles en route to their demise. The castles contained dungeons. The dungeons were too dark to take pictures. The stories were too dreadful as I learned from the guide that two hundred people would be housed in one of the rooms of the dungeons, a room that could barely hold twenty. The women were separated from the men and were housed in their own quarters.

For those who were classified as troublemakers, they would be crammed in a room with a small window located far above. Once the high tides came in, the tides would hit against the walls and the room would soon fill up with water as water gushed through the only open window and these unwilling future slaves would drown. Also, no matter which room they occupied, these men and women targeted as slaves were forced to live in their own feces.

The remains of those who died in these dungeons are what constitute the floors today. When stepping into these rooms, the floors are extremely soft from dead bodies, human waste and moisture. To experience this was morbid, quite eerie and unsettling. During this trip, I discovered that the British did not capture these Africans by themselves. The white man was actually assisted by other Africans. Basically, it was the Fanti tribe of Cape Coast who captured the Ga and other tribes throughout Africa and vehemently brought them to this dreadful place. I am not sure if there was an ultimatum over the Fanti's head. Capture or be captured. But they participated nevertheless.

The second floor of the Cape Coast castle was a much different world and environment. These were the quarters for the white people who were indeed foreigners. They lived like kings and queens compared to our African people. The floors were not made of human bodies, but were wooden floors that are still preserved today. These quarters had all the necessary amenities. I could not help feel pain in this place. This is one of the many castles located on the shores of the Atlantic where some of my ancestors sailed, died, and struggled.

Only the strong were chosen to go on the slave ships and the strongest of them would be sold for the highest price. They exited to the ships from a door that was marked "Door of No Return." This mandatory trip away from their homeland was determined to be and was in fact their final trip across the waters. I can happily say that since then this door has been renamed the "Door of Return" to welcome African descendants back to the motherland.

Back to Hempstead and New Haven, I will build my story and my research about Hempstead from this premise. I am more than sure that freedom may not have been how our Jackson ancestors entered this land. However, it is extremely necessary that we embrace the thought of free people of color for a good number of our people during the time of slavery as it ended in the North and continued in the South. Grandma Ro was closer to the situation than we were but she may have had limited information about her great-grandparents. After all, we didn't know much more about our great-ancestors until now when records have become more accessible. For a very long time, we weren't that interested in the past as we focused more toward the present and our future.

One thing is for sure though. Grandma had to have had other than Madagascan in her blood since her mother, a mulatto from Washington DC, supposedly had mixed blood. But she didn't talk about that at all. Her children, my aunt and my father, appear to have been aware of this but it was not fully developed with us. My father never wanted us to lose sight of the fact that we are African Americans. Grandma's mother carried the Madagascan seed as part of her African ancestry. I really do not know the African origin of many of our people. Through DNA, traces of our African ancestry are beginning to surface. On the African side, we originated from places like Madagascar, Senegal, Sierra Leone, and Ghana, and we are mixed with West Indian, Bahamian, for sure. Also, more research may indicate which ships and nations landed where in each state and which nationalities may have been imported from those boats.

I remember when I was a teen Grandma Ro told me that she had information about her ancestry in her attic or on the third floor, and she suggested that I read through the documents. I was too busy growing up. Those documents may have been the key to uncover even more information. I do know now for certain that Grandma Ro's paternal grandparents had moved from New York to New Haven, Connecticut. New Haven may have been the place where these ancestors originated on the Jackson side. Some on our ancestors on the main ancestral line were born and raised on Long Island in the mid-1700s or even before. Nevertheless, when Grandma was born, her paternal grandmother and her great-grandparents had already passed. It appears that her paternal grandfather was living at least through 1910 or even later.

Grandma Ro may have been eleven or a little older when second great-grandfather William passed and may not have had the opportunity to speak to him extensively about our prior ancestors and his place of birth. What was shared with her was the fact that she was Madagascan, and she carried that heritage with great pride. As for us, we have to depend on records and those things that we were told or already know. However, there were in fact rocks that had not been turned over even by our parents and grandparents. Many of our ancestors have now been properly identified in this genealogical research.

As stated previously, I am not sure if freedom holds true for Grandma's great-grandparents who are clearly noted as born in New York. The question is when did my African ancestors from the Jackson seed first land on these shores? Third great-grandfather Semon Jackson was born in about 1787. His parents probably close to the 1750s. His parents may have been born in New Haven. Though I have not yet located any records to support the move from New Haven to Hempstead, later records do show that my second great-grandparents William and Henrietta relocated from Hempstead to New Haven. Records show that slavery in New York began in 1655, and it was totally abolished there in 1827, but gradually since approximately 1820. Our third great-grandparents were in Hempstead at the time of slavery and our fourth great-grandparents were there as well.

The 1850 federal census for Hempstead, New York, lists William H. Jackson among those with the surname Jackson. Second great-grandfather William H. Jackson, born about 1831, is listed along with his father, Semon Jackson (b. abt. 1787 or 1788), his brother Charles Jackson (b. 1828), probably a sister-in-law (wife to his brother Charles) Angeline Jackson (b. 1827) and their two children, Catherine Jackson, a newborn and Edgar Jackson who is eight. They are free inhabitants. The wife of Semon is absent from the household at the time of the census or her information may be contained on the next page of the census that is not visible. Again, the 1850 census didn't identify family relationships anyway. His wife, my third great-grandmother, was in fact Leonora Jackson born about 1787, and she is located in the 1870 census with her son Charles and two young children.

In summary, Madagascar is indeed a part of our ancestry. Those from Ethiopia and Somalia have often sensed this. My sister and son have close friends from these areas who immigrated to Washington DC. One of my first cousins Johnnie Jackson is or was married to either an Ethiopian or a Somalian, and he lives in Washington DC, a place where many immigrants over the past several decades now live. Some years ago, when we would clarify our Madagascan heritage to Somalians, some stated that we are all cousins. This proves true from the DNA sampling that shows our ancestry on Grandma Ro's maternal lineage as having the Ethiopian halotype. Even without the DNA testing, we know somehow that we are kin and from at least a portion of the same seed.

Choosing the Family Surname

Contrary to the misconception that slaves in the South and other places took the names of their masters, research reveals that the slaves arbitrarily chose their own surnames, oftentimes after presidents. Others chose the name of a former owner, a famous person, or someone who was locally respected. Again, adopting the name of the slaveholder was not the common occurrence in the South except in cases where the slaveholder was the birth father. If the slaves were on the run, they definitely didn't want to adopt the name of their slaveholder. That would have made it easy for them to be located, captured and returned to the one from whom they escaped. They were a lot smarter than that. One thing is for sure, we can pretty much bet that the American names of our early ancestors were different from their given surnames on the shores of Africa to include the first name in most, if not all, instances.[61] This may not have held true for the slaves in Hempstead and probably New Haven who may have taken the master's name when they were freed.[62] Very little information has surfaced to support this.

As far as the Jackson family, it should be noted that one of the wealthy landowners in Hempstead and in Connecticut was named Robert Jackson, a white man. He was among other very wealthy men who were part of a congregation in Stamford, Connecticut, most of them being natives of England. They bought the Hempstead territory through a treaty with the Indians who originally owned and inhabited the land. By the 1850 census, there were quite a few persons with the surname Jackson, both black and white, among this small population of less than sixty slaveholders in Hempstead.

Race was included in the 1850 census, and our Jackson family was identified as black. Second great-grandfather William forever carried his middle initial *H* and is located with this initial in the 1850 census and on quite a few other records, to include draft records and the census in subsequent years. It appears that some people decided to adopt the name of one of the wealthiest persons on Hempstead and maybe in Connecticut as well and that person may or may not have been their particular slaveholder. Others may have been his direct kin. There is absolutely no record that we were anywhere related to the white Robert Jackson. It just doesn't seem probable for the Jackson seed. Again, my Jackson descendants who were located were forever listed as black though, ironically, my great-uncle Alex spoke so eloquently with a recognizable British accent that caused him to stand out. Now that I have learned that the Jackson seed or a portion thereof first arrived in New Haven, Connecticut, in the late sixteenth or early seventeenth century, new and improved information may change some of this scenario. But that happens anyway as more descendants read the document or get together and add information that they know firsthand or that was shared with them throughout the years. To date, these are the things uncovered. Changes may indeed occur.

Jackson was one of the most widely used surnames among the overall population in Hempstead, among both black and white people. Fortunately, in 1850, the inhabitants were distinguished by color or race separating one Jackson from the other. On Long Island, during this period of time, there were a number of other widely used surnames such as Abrams, Bailey, Baldwin, Combs, to name a few.[63] Checking the last names of presidents that served during or before 1850, there is no widely used president's name. So using a president's surname was not the case for our ancestors in the North. Furthermore, in the 1850 census, the surname Washington is not found at all, and the surnames Adams, Jefferson, and Harrison only had one or two persons with that name in Hempstead at that time. So the theory that president's names were often used by former slaves did not hold true in Hempstead, though it may have held true in the South. In Hempstead, no president by the last name Jackson had yet served as president. Again, it is known that the surname Jackson in our bloodline was definitely adopted in Connecticut and was also used by our progenitors in Hempstead.

Surnames are important identifiers in one's genealogy. So are middle names. With the proper surname, I am able to trace some of my family back as far as the fifth and sixth great-grandparents and others cannot be traced further than the third or fourth. As far as how the last name for most of our ancestors occurred is hard to explain at this point with the exception of the surname Dubois. The surname Dubois originated from one of my forefathers, a white Frenchman who was a physician who brought his mixed Bahamian sons born to a slave mistress to the United States. Alexander and John Dubois were his sons who fourth great-grandfather James cared for and brought back to the states with him.

As for the others, I do believe they had the choice to take any name they wanted, and they chose Hatcher, Jackson, Odrick, Riddle, and Frisby, which the latter three are odd names for the African American. Moore, Jones, Brooks, Brown, and probably other names if we were able to trace all the female side by maiden name are also surnames among our heritage. I don't think any president's surnames are identifiable in our ancestry though. Based on the aforementioned, the assumption that African Americans used the surnames of their owners is mostly not true and this assumption may be mostly false for many slaves. However, it is quite possible that one of the surnames may have originated from a white man who fathered a black child or the mother may have been white and the father black. The mother of that mixed child may be unknown. Again, it is hard to tell which surnames were assigned in that manner. Other family names may have been names chosen by occupation and may have been derived from a foreign name and may have even been misspelled. No matter how they were acquired, these surnames along with a racial identifier are critical in the search for one's people.

Our Jackson Ancestors Relocate from Hempstead to New Haven

Second great-grandparents William H. Jackson and Henrietta L. Jackson relocated from Hempstead to New Haven sometime after 1850. The 1865 census shows that he was working in New Haven as a school janitor and later as a messenger, a very special governmental appointment. They are living with their children, great-grandaunt Henrietta, who was named after her mother, second great-granduncle Benjamin, and my great-grandfather Robert. In 1865, second great-grandmother, Henrietta, passes and Charlotte Howard, a mulatto, moves or had moved from New York to New Haven to help care for the family. The 1880 census shows that Charlotte Howard is living as a housekeeper in the home with William along with his son Robert. The other children are already grown. William eventually takes Charlotte as his lawfully wedded wife. I do not believe they had any children together.

I am so overjoyed and extremely happy about this recent finding. In 1874, William Jackson, an African American, was appointed messenger in the Court of Common Pleas.[64] This is without a doubt my second great-grandfather, and I am pleased with his accomplishment during times when such opportunities were few.

Again, not much had been shared with us about our ancestors on Hempstead. It may not have held great importance at the time since the Jackson seed originated in New Haven as we were often told. However, finding many key and directly related ancestors who were born in Hempstead is one of the biggest surprises on my family tree. What is not surprising is that our ancestors were Madagascan on at least my grandmother's maternal side. As I have mentioned often in this document, our Madagascan ancestry had been mentioned often to us.

Yet someone in the family knew about Hempstead because my grandmother's brother spent a lot of time on Hempstead, had a son who was actually born in Connecticut, probably Bridgeport or possibly New Haven, but still lives in Hempstead today. So moving back and forth between Connecticut and Long Island must not have been uncommon. When you think about it, even my immediate family traveled back and forth on a constant basis to visit. The distance wasn't far at all. The southern shores of Connecticut and the tip of Long Island were only a stone's throw from each other and a boat ride away. I am told by members of our Hempstead family that great-uncle Alexander visited other family members with the surname Jackson who lived in Hempstead during the time that I was old enough to know but did not know. And this is a fact. I must say that I am elated and honored to know what I know now.

Next, I will summarize the story about the life of second great-grandfather William H. Jackson though some facts may have been previously addressed.

Summary of Second Great-Grandfather William's Life

At the age of nineteen, second great-grandfather William H. Jackson (born abt. 1831) is listed in the 1850 federal census in Hempstead, Long Island, New York, and he is a free man. In 1850, he is living in the same household as his father, Semon Jackson, age sixty-two, who was born in 1787 in New York. They are listed as black. Others in the household are William's brother Charles, age twenty-two, his sister-in-law Angeline, age twenty-one, and their children Edgar, age eight and Catherine, a newborn. His mother is later located and her name is Leonora Jackson who is born in approximately the same year as her husband, Semon. She too is listed as black. In the US civil war Draft Records of 1863-'65, great-grandfather William is registered as living in Connecticut, black, married, and born in New York.

In 1860, the census shows second great-grandfather William married to second great-grandmother Henrietta L. Jackson (b. 1836) also born in New York. I was unable to determine second great-grandmother's maiden name. There are others on the island with the first name Henrietta with years of birth close to hers, but I have not determined which one was second great-grandmother. I do know from the census that both second great-grandparents were born in New York.

Second great-grandparents William and Henrietta are living in New Haven, Connecticut, with a one-year-old child Henrietta (b. 1859) who is named after her mother. By 1870, two more children are born: Benjamin W. (b. 1858) and Robert H (b. 1856). As stated earlier, living with them as a housekeeper is Charlotte Howard, a mulatto from New York. Somewhere during this time period, second great-grandmother Henrietta has passed. By 1880, second great-grandfather William is married to Charlotte Howard Jackson (b. 1842), and seventeen year old Robert is living with them. In 1892, it appears that William H. Jackson is back in Hempstead, New York. His second wife may have gone on to the Lord and his children are all grown. If he in fact returned to Hempstead and if this is the right person, he is listed with the occupation "Gentleman." Otherwise, he may have passed in New Haven as well. I will continue to search for more definitive documents, if they exist.

Great-Grandparents Robert Henry Jackson and Madame Henrietta Frisby Jackson

"The fear of the Lord is the beginning of knowledge" (Proverbs 1:7). Great-grandfather Robert Henry Jackson (b. February 1863) was the youngest child of second great-grandparents William and Henrietta Jackson. He was born in New Haven, Connecticut, and married great-grandmother, the former Henrietta Louise Frisby, who was born in July 1876 in Washington DC. Great-grandmother Henrietta's mother, my second great-grandmother Elizabeth Brooks (b. 1851), was born in Washington DC as well. She was listed as a mulatto. Great-grandmother Henrietta's father, my second great-grandfather, Joseph Frisby was born in Philadelphia, Pennsylvania, in 1846, and he was also listed as a mulatto.

Great-grandparents Robert and Henrietta had two children, Romietta and Alexander. Romietta Leonora Jackson (Grandma Ro) was born May 27, 1899, in Oakland, California. Great-uncle Alexander L. Jackson was born in 1902 in New Haven, Connecticut.

"Praise the Lord with harp; sing unto him with the psaltery and an instrument of ten strings" (Psalm 33:2). As stated earlier, great-grandmother Henrietta was known as Madame Henrietta Frisby Jackson, and she was an understudy for Madame Sissieretta Jones, a well-know opera star. It is great-grandmother Henrietta who brings the musical DNA to this family though my mother's family was musically inclined as well. Her daughter, Grandma Ro, was a well-known classical pianist in New Haven and Grandma Ro's daughter, my aunt Natalie, was musically talented and well-known as an opera singer as was stated earlier about her career as a vocalist. Second great-grandmother Henrietta had a brother, second great-granduncle William, born abt. 1879. He also was born in Washington DC.

In 1880 at age seventeen, great-grandfather Robert lived with his father and stepmother Charlotte, and he was attending school. Around 1898 he and great-grandmother Henrietta married, and they had their first child, Romietta, in 1899. His occupation in the 1890 census is "Steward at the Elks' Club" in Rutland, Vermont. His wife, the former Henrietta Frisby, is enumerated as a "singer." How long they stayed there, I do not know, but by the next census they are living in New Haven where he worked also as a steward for the Elks Club and then as a messenger. Their second and youngest child, great-uncle Alex was born in New Haven, Connecticut, a couple of years later. So I assume their tour in Rutland, where jobs were likely flourishing, was not that long.

As stated earlier, great-grandmother Henrietta (b. 1876) was born to Joseph Frisby (b. 1846) who was born in Philadelphia, Pennsylvania, and Elizabeth Brooks, born 1851 in Washington DC. They are all listed as mulatto.

Second great-grandfather Joseph Frisby's mother and father, like him, were born in Philadelphia, Pennsylvania. In the 1850 census, second great-grandfather Joseph Frisby is enumerated as living in Philadelphia, Pennsylvania, at the age of five, as a "free black," and the family is listed as mulatto. He is living with his grandmother, fourth great-grandmother Mintie Frisby, a fifty-five-year-old black female who was born in Delaware in 1795. She was the wife to my fourth great-grandfather who I believe to be James Frisby who was born in Philadelphia in 1795 and died on December 6, 1847, in Philadelphia. Also, living in the household is third great-grandfather George Frisby (b. 1820), age thirty, who worked as a porter and is the father to second great-grandfather Joseph and his brothers. Second great-grandfather George was born in Philadelphia, Pennsylvania, in 1820 and died on March 29, 1898, at the age of seventy-nine. The other occupants of the house are two other small children also born in Philadelphia, Pennsylvania. They are second great-grandfather Joseph's brothers, my second great-granduncles Charles (b. 1847) and Tracis (b. 1846).

Great-grandmother Henrietta's mother was the former Elizabeth Brooks, born 1851 in Washington DC. Both of second great-grandmother Elizabeth's parents, my third great-grandparents, were born in Baltimore, Maryland, and second great-grandmother Elizabeth was baptized December 1, 1851, in Christ Church Parish, located at Chase and St. Paul Streets, Baltimore, Maryland. Her parents were third great-grandparents Henry Brooks (b. 1817) and Henrietta Brooks (b. 1825), after whom our great-grandmother Henrietta was named.

In 1850 our third great-grandparents Henry and Henrietta owned land in Washington DC. They had fifteen children with five children living to include second great-grandmother Elizabeth (b. 1851) and her siblings: Margaret Brooks (b. 1843), Julius Brooks (b. 1854), Alexander Brooks (b. 1860) and Georgiana Brooks (b. 1864). There were children born to these children. Second great-grandmother Elizabeth had five children and two lived: Henrietta and William. Third great-grandmother Henrietta is still living at the time of the 1900 census, making her seventy-six years old, and second great-grandmother Elizabeth appears to be widowed, and she is forty-nine. She and second great-grandfather Joseph had been married for twenty-five years. He was around fifty-five when he passed.

Second great-grandfather Joseph's mother was deceased at the time of the 1850 census and his father is listed as widowed. In his later years, second great-grandfather Joseph continues to be listed as a mulatto. He is a waiter in a hotel and both of his parents were born in Philadelphia, Pennsylvania, as well. This is great-grandmother Henrietta's family that more than likely carried the Madagascan seed on her mother's side at least. In summary, great-grandmother Henrietta was a professional opera singer, a mulatto, the daughter to Joseph and Elizabeth, a sister to William, a wife to Robert, and a mother to Romietta and Alexander. I am told that she died early and great-grandfather remarried and left the New Haven area.

Moving Toward the South; First Stop Philadelphia, then Delaware, Baltimore, and Washington DC

E ven though I know of others who have kin in New Jersey, I have no direct family members that I know of that were born or ever lived there. Therefore, this journey will proceed with the first stop being Philadelphia, Pennsylvania, where a number of my ancestors were born or where others lived. As you read earlier, fourth great-grandfather is assumed to be the James Frisby who was born in Philadelphia, Pennsylvania, in about 1785 and died there on December 6, 1847. His death preceded the 1850 census where his wife, his son and his son's children appear. He was married to my fourth great-grandmother Mintie Frisby also born about 1785 and her birthplace is listed as Delaware, probably Wilmington or Dover or some other developing city. She is definitely located in the 1850 census living with her family in Philadelphia, Pennsylvania.

Fourth great-grandparents James and Mintie had children with George Frisby being one of them. Third great-grandfather George was born in Philadelphia in 1820. He worked as a porter in Philadelphia and appears in the 1850 census with his mother and his sons, my second great-grandfather Joseph Frisby being one of his children. Third great-grandfather George was listed as widowed and his wife, second great-grandfather Joseph's mother, must have passed away at the time of the 1850 census. For now her name is unknown. His son Joseph was my second great-grandfather and father to my great-grandmother, Mme. Henrietta Frisby Jackson, who was born in Washington DC. Second great-grandfather Joseph had moved to Washington DC from Philly, and he married third great-grandmother Elizabeth who was born in Washington DC along with their children.

During these times, the fastest mode of transportation was the train. After a period of time, African Americans were becoming a lot more mobile as they moved outside of their comfort zone and started meeting and marrying people from other places. African Americans were already on the move since the early 1800s either as runaway slaves using the Underground Railroad or they were born free due to one of their parents being a white free person.

In 1800 through 1830, Philadelphia was the largest city in America. It was a burgeoning city and home to a number of immigrants. The Dutch and Swedes were the earliest settlers and as usual the Indians already dwelt on this land. The Indians watched the development of this city as buildings were being constructed, and they sold their game and venison from the neighboring wild.[65] There were quite a few surrounding towns that existed around Philadelphia. These towns eventually came under one municipal government in 1854.[66]

But what was it like for an African American in this "City of Brotherly Love." According to research regarding the emancipation of slaves in Pennsylvania, indentured servants and slaves were being freed in the 1700s in order to become a part of a newly established wage labor system.[67] Slaves and indentured servants were the property of their masters and had to be kept with room and board for lack of better words. We can assume that such amenities were perhaps extremely inferior for most. Unlike the master's responsibilities to the slaves under the slave system, under the newly-established wage labor system each man was responsible for his own welfare. Based on this, it was cheaper for the master not to have to keep his help as slaves and servants. Immigrants were becoming a major part of Philadelphia, and they worked for a much lower pay rate than others already inhabitants of this country.

In 1780, an act was passed in Pennsylvania to gradually free the slaves, but the indentured form of servitude still existed. This indentured servitude was not limited to blacks and mulattos, but clearly included Indian, German, Irish, Dutch, and Scottish indentured slaves and servants. So understand this right now, though I am trying not to be too rigid, when someone white refers to you as a product of slavery, call them the same back. Everyone was not free and this whole economic system was about the economy and the wealth of a few white men and their families.

The bottom line is that whites were in servitude just like us in America. Immigrants and poor whites did what they had to do to survive, and they may have appeared for a long time on the slave schedules as did the African American. In Philadelphia, the indentured slaves were overwhelmingly domestic and most women worked in the private households as maids, tutors, and they raised the children.[68]

In Philadelphia, Quakers continued to be a major force in the abolitionist movement in favor of the dissolution of the cruel institution of slavery. The Quakers had already set their slaves free. As for the two systems listed above, there was a fine line between indentured servants and slavery. But masters could still beat and punish the servants just like the slaves, but they had to follow the State law when doing so. Overall, servants were more desirable to the white establishment than slaves because the cost was cut in half to purchase a servant and it was cheaper to provide care for him or her. This cheaper cost was the only reason slaves were being freed by the establishment, but they were in fact freed into a different kind of servitude.

As late as 1820, three fourths of young African American men and almost 60 percent of the African American women in Philadelphia worked in the white households.[69] By 1840, only sixty-four slaves were left in the whole state of Pennsylvania down considerably from the 796 slaves living in the state in 1810. The men in control were bona fide con men and swindlers. They freed the slaves and then indentured them. What made it even more complicated and unfair is that, during this time period, African Americans were not allowed to learn a trade or do anything else to increase their wealth. After they finished their five to seven year service as indentured slaves, they were limited to working as cottagers, a rural labor system for marginal whites and blacks whose homes were cottages, and their ability to gain wealth and independence was limited.[70]

Other things of importance occurred in this city in these earlier times. Benjamin Franklin discovered the light bulb in the mid-1700s. In 1816, gas as an illumination was introduced. In the 1830s and 1840s, Philadelphia had all the makings of a big city and little resemblance to brotherly love. The city of Philadelphia was in constant turmoil.[71] Because of its factories, immigrants came to Philadelphia in large numbers from Ireland and Germany. Because of the large immigration of Irish and Germans, Philadelphia came under attack and was victimized by fires and riots. Most buildings were made of logs and these buildings could not survive these fires. Buildings actually burned to the ground.

The Irish were the main focus of the riots because of their Catholic belief that angered the majority of the people in America who were mainly Protestants. The Irish's spiritual focus was very much different from the rest of the population. There was confusion and uproar because only the King James Version (KJV) of the Bible was allowed to be read, and reading from the KJV Bible was mandatory in the public schools. The Irish, who were Catholic, resented the fact that the Catholic Bible was prohibited from use.

In a nutshell, the majority of the people in Philadelphia were very much against the infiltration of the Irish (and Germans) who were coming in large numbers. Also, since the Irish were Catholics, a lot of the controversy surrounded their religious belief, resulting in these riots being labeled "the Philadelphia Bible Riots." Anything Irish was being burned to the ground and the Catholic churches were the major targets of these riotous discourses. A lot of property was damaged as a result of these riots, but few lives were lost even though the Irish had no protection offered to them by the city. In spite of these things, the Irish survived.[72]

Among other things, Philadelphia consisted of wood-yards, boat builders and mast makers on the river fronts and sea captains and seafaring men. Farmer markets were set up in certain areas for the wholesale trade in butter, eggs, poultry, meats, vegetables, and other products of the farms of the adjacent country.[73] Farmer markets still exist today and the Lancaster, Pennsylvania, farmers from Pennsylvania's Dutch country sell the best and freshest food products in the world. Retail stores were also being established and a big city was under way.

As much as things change, they remain the same. What particularly caught my eye, because of the mixed racial makeup of my ancestors who were born in Philadelphia, were the laws that were in place to address marriage and fornication between blacks and whites. Marriage and fornication between blacks and whites were illegal acts. If caught in such a relationship, the black person was punished much more severely than the white counterpart. No surprises here. Research and records indicate that though marriage was prohibited, fornication continued at an all time high as evidenced by Philadelphia's burgeoning mulatto population.[74] Historical documents indicate that there were so many mulattos being birthed in Philadelphia.

My ancestors were definitely a part of this phenomenon. I still do not know if part of my ancestry is Irish, German, Dutch, or Scottish. For sure, the census did not capture the ethnic make-up of the mulatto. The enumerator came to this conclusion based on the physical appearance of the African mixed-person with no questions asked about the actual ethnicities involved. From this mixing, our race developed and that is why we are African Americans today, some with very little mixture to none and others with more. In fact, I have noticed recently that famous African Americans are beginning to simply identify their nationality as American, if born here. The race is often not listed since the race is mostly obvious from their photos unless a person's parents are of dual race. Even then there are a number of surprises because the person of mixed ancestry more often than not looks like an African American.

Slavery in Pennsylvania was abolished in 1780 but the abolition of slavery was gradual just like in other states. In addition, the restrictive laws in place in Pennsylvania no longer applied to those already listed as free. But like the rest of America, the freed or free persons of color were prohibited from serving in the state militia due to the restrictive antebellum laws or from voting.

Between 1790 and 1830, it is reported that the economic conditions of African Americans were beginning to improve and a number of African Americans had finally reached a point of comfort and even purchased real estate. Poor whites became jealous, and they were antagonized by the advancement of the African American. Similar to what was occurring in New Haven, Connecticut, organized white labor efforts were under way to block African Americans from gaining or keeping paying jobs.[75] Furthermore, Philadelphia was an important stop for the Underground Railroad. The influx of a number of runaway slaves in this area as well as the blocking of jobs from African Americans only led to crime and other problems for the city. No jobs, increased crime. It seems to go hand and hand. You can't have things both ways. This is Philadelphia, the city of brotherly love.

My ancestors were born and lived up and down the East Coast but not farther south than North Carolina and only in places on the East Coast. My second and third great-grandfathers on the Frisby side of my ancestry were born in Philadelphia in 1820 and 1845, respectively. Records clearly indicate that my ancestors born in Philadelphia were free and mulatto. Without a doubt, some had been fathered or mothered by other than those with African ancestry. This was definitely not an uncommon phenomenon in the city of Philadelphia. The birth of mixed children was pretty heavy duty. The most stringent prohibition of marriage and fornication between blacks and whites contained in the law could not stop this from happening. Now that's brotherly love.

I finally know some of the story. It feels a whole lot better knowing that some of our European mixture was the result of love and not by force. After all, Philadelphia is translated to mean "brotherly love" and is one of the four types of love found in the Bible. These types of love are translated from the Greek words as follows. Specifically, "phileo" refers to common love for those who naturally get along and have common interests. Agape is the highest form of love out of the four types of spiritual love and it is the ultimate supernatural love. This type of love is selfless, sacrificial, and unconditional love as defined by the Bible. In the Gospel according to John 14:21, Jesus commands us to keep the commandments to show our unconditional love toward him. Jesus goes on to say that if we love him, we will be loved by our Father. Further, if we love Jesus, he will show up in our lives. Therefore, love God and love thy neighbors as thyself.

The other types of love are eros meaning "self-gratifying and selfish with no care or concern for others," and astorgos is the type of love shown specifically to family members. It is the love between brothers and sisters. The ultimate and most powerful love, agape love, comes from God. Love God and love your neighbors are the royal commandments.

But what remains obscure is the ethnicity of the Europeans who are a part of me. Were they German, Irish, Dutch, Swedes, or some others who had immigrated to America and lived in the places where my African ancestry lived? I may never know the full facts, yet I have to accept this and no matter what I will forever be black. Alleluia and Amen.

The census of 1850 lists my third great-grandfather, George Frisby, living in Philadelphia, and he is employed as a porter. He and his family were free people of color. His father was born in approximately 1785 and, at some point, may have been an indentured slave or servant. I really don't know. According to records, his mother, Mintie, was born in 1785 in Delaware, and she is listed as black, and she too could have been indentured or of mixed ancestry. But her children and her children's children are listed as mulatto, and they were born in Philadelphia, Pennsylvania, to a mulatto father and both of the grandchildren's parents were born in Philadelphia, Pennsylvania as well. My second great-grandfather, Joseph Frisby, is one of those grandchildren, and he was born in 1845. In a later census, he is listed as a waiter in a hotel.

From at least 1820 forward or even before, my ancestors were born and living in Philadelphia as free people, and they were mulatto and simply by their steady employment enjoyed the benefits of such. This is what I have learned about my ancestors from Philadelphia so far.

Others who moved to Philadelphia from Connecticut were those who were part of the Dubois seed. A couple of my second great-granduncles moved from Waterbury and Cheshire, Connecticut, to Philadelphia and at least one married a woman who was born there. A number of their children were born in Philadelphia as well. One of my second great-granduncles, James Dubois, remained there and his children lived and died there. At least one of my second great-granduncles, John Dubois, returned to Connecticut, his state of birth, to live in Waterbury, Connecticut, with his other brothers who had married women from Bermuda. His brothers may have moved for a period of time to Bermuda, but they definitely moved back and lived in Waterbury. At least two of the brothers' children were born in Bermuda. Three of their sisters lived in Waterbury with their spouses as well. My grandfather also lived in Philly.

My grandfather, Theodore William Hatcher Sr., who was born in Waterbury and lived in New Haven in his adult years and attended Yale, moved to the wealthy town of Haverford, Pennsylvania, located about ten miles west of Philadelphia and then he moved to Philadelphia. He had separated from his wife, my Grandma Ro. Prior to that they had two children who were born and who lived in New Haven, my father and my aunt. Again, I have quite a few old photos of Granddaddy where he served as a butler for an attorney in this wealthy town of Haverford and then as a chauffeur. I just remember that he had joyous times in Philadelphia, and he was always happy when we saw him. His favorite times were when he was involved with the Elks, and he often attended their conferences and other festive events.

At a young age, my father moved to Philadelphia with his father. My grandfather had gained custody of his son. My aunt remained in New Haven with their mother. My aunt Natalie recalls the pain of this separation so vividly even today. She said the day her brother was taken from her, she recalls crying for a very long time. However, he returned in the summers to spend time with her and their mother. Grandma Ro must have had visitation rights. Dad and Aunt Natalie would also spend time with their paternal grandmother in Waterbury. But my father lived the rest of the year with the Judge family and their children in Media, Pennsylvania, which was not far from where his father lived. This allowed him to be raised around other children. Granddaddy and Pop Judge were best of friends.

Spending his summers in New Haven kept Dad in close touch with his family. His cousin Katherine remembers him well when she was only four. So that meant he was about thirteen. She advised me that she was so very fond of him to the point of having a crush on him when she was a young girl. Her mother, his Aunt Mabel who was married to his Uncle Alex, was extremely fond of her nephew as well. He was so special to and loved by all of them. The move appeared to have been emotionally hard for everyone in Connecticut including my dad. Nevertheless, after graduating from high school in Media, Dad attended Lincoln University for three full years before he was drafted into the army that disrupted his studies. When he was discharged from the army, he returned to Connecticut.

Delaware

I know of only one ancestor born in Delaware. That would be my fourth great-grandmother Mintie, born about 1785. She married my fourth great-grandfather who I believe to be James Frisby from Philadelphia, Pennsylvania, and she lived in Philly for the rest of her life. She can be located in the 1850 census that indicates that she was a free person of color. This census preceded the passing of the Emancipation Proclamation.

According to information regarding slavery in the state of Delaware, Delaware was a slave state that decided to join the Union in its effort to free the slaves. This colony depended heavily on Indian slaves, but diseases and westward migration had already emptied the region of native tribes.[76] Once the Dutch took over this colony, African slaves were purchased first from the West Indies and then from Africa. Delaware originally had a labor-intensive tobacco and corn economy. Wheat that was not as labor-intensive became a major cash crop and didn't require the hard labor of the slaves. So slavery began to diminish in Delaware particularly in the northern part of this small state. The Quakers and abolitionists were very active here as well.

Debates occurred between those in the northern part of this colony comprised mainly of abolitionists and those in the southern part who supported slavery and needed this institution for its economy. In 1790, the slaves made up 70 percent of the state's population, so I would imagine that fourth great-grandmother's parents could have possibly been in that count or they had already traveled through the underground and had found freedom. I do not have any record of her parents, and therefore, I may never know what actually occurred. Within time, Delaware had a population of free blacks but the establishment still depended on them for hard labor just as other states did.

Many African Americans passed secretly through the colonies on the eastern shores by way of the Underground Railroad. There were many good and caring white people who helped them along the way via safe havens in their homes and in their barns. They also allowed the slaves to use their roads. Delaware was the "last stop to freedom." The most memorable quote I have read about Delaware reads as follows: "When I found I had crossed that line, I looked at my hands to see if I was the same person. There was such a glory over everything" (Harriet Tubman).[77]

The trail for the Underground Railroad ushered slaves to freedom, and Harriet Tubman excelled as "conductor" of this railroad. The trail was extremely dangerous. Swamps and marshes were used to hide the slaves from those who sought them. This trip was unreal and very risky. Some actually survived this perilous passage. Others did not. Slaves were often very tired and hungry during this clandestine trip in search of freedom and white supporters gave them a place to rest and food to eat before they advanced further by the paths identified as the Underground Railroad. In addition to avoiding capture, the runaway slaves had a lot of worries along the way. Some came down with diseases caused mainly by insects. They had to fear and avoid snakes and wild animals. Some even drowned in the swamps. But others made it to the promise land and beyond.

Maryland and the Escape to Freedom

Maryland was settled in 1634, and most Africans and mulattos were indentured servants and not slaves.[78] At the point where the tobacco industry was booming, those whites who were in control found it necessary to change the status of Africans, mulattos, and Indians from indentured to enslaved servants for the protection of the tobacco industry. They needed to enforce more control to ensure that they were prosperous, and they cared less about anyone else's welfare and happiness. Most slaves worked as field hands and were often separated from their families. They worked night and day to the point of exhaustion. As usual, others were enslaved for the sole purpose of hard work and solely for the masters' benefit. But things have a way of coming back to haunt those who are selfish, cunning, and cruel. In spite of the rich soil and climate in the county of Prince George, Maryland, where tobacco was grown, the tobacco industry dwindled, and Maryland found no further need for the slaves. They wanted the slaves gone from their state and undertook efforts to make that happen. They wanted them to go back to Africa.[79]

Third great-grandparents Henry and Henrietta Brooks were born in Baltimore, Maryland, in 1817 and 1825, respectively, and there were fifteen children born to this union with five living to include second great-grandmother Elizabeth (b. 1851) and her siblings: Julius Brooks (b. 1854), Alexander Brooks (b. 1860), Georgianna Brooks (b. 1865), and Arnold Brooks (b. unknown). I located three of the ten siblings who had passed with two who appeared to have been a twin to two of the surviving children at the time. They were Margaret Brooks (b. 1849), James H. Brooks (b. 1851) and Anna Brooks (b. 1860).

Second great-grandmother, Elizabeth Brooks was born in Washington DC in 1851 and probably most of her siblings were born there as well. Her parents moved to Washington DC from Baltimore and in 1850 third great-grandparents Henry and Henrietta Brooks owned land in and around Washington DC. They like other families in our ancestry were listed as mulattos, and they were free. I do not know the names of my fourth great-grandparents or their place of origin at this time.

Second great-grandmother, the former Elizabeth Brooks, married Joseph Frisby, and they were the parents to my great-grandmother Mme. Henrietta Frisby Jackson. She was named after her grandmother, Henrietta Brooks, whose origin or that of her mother and possibly her father may have been Madagascar. Second great-grandparents Elizabeth and Joseph had five children and two lived: Henrietta and William Perry Frisby. Third great-grandmother Henrietta was still living at the time of the 1900 census, making her seventy-five or seventy-six years old. She and her daughter, second great-grandmother Elizabeth, were both widowed. Our second great-grandparents had been married for twenty-five years and second great-grandfather Joseph appears to have died at the age of fifty-five. During the 1910 census, second great-grandmother Elizabeth moved to New Haven, Connecticut, to be with her daughter, Mme. Henrietta Frisby Jackson, who became very ill and who died from a brain disease caused by injury or stroke.

I am not sure how long some of our ancestors may have continued to live in Baltimore. I do know that Baltimore, Maryland, is where my mother was born when her mother and father moved there from North Carolina with their two sons. They lived at 18 E. Hamilton Street located in the downtown area of Baltimore, Maryland. The multifamily property was built in 1820, and it still stands today.

My mother's father, Joseph "Allen" Jones, died when she was about two years old. My mother told me that her father was known for his excellent masonry and his name was engraved on a few structures that may still exist in North Carolina where he lived and worked as a young man. Grandfather Allen's death was a shock to the children and their mother, who was my grandmother, Fannie Moore Jones. After his death, my grandmother and her children moved to Waterbury, Connecticut, where most of her sisters lived. We called her Nana. She remarried but had no children with her second husband. She married Charles Cross who was a wonderful stepfather to her children and a wonderful grandfather to us.

Entering the South: Virginia

Fairfax County, Virginia

Slavery in the South has been very well documented over the years, making it unnecessary to do a great amount of research about the surrounding events during that time. My ancestors in the South were born in Virginia and North Carolina where the first slave ships originally landed. The first twenty "Negroes," seventeen men and three women, were transported across the Atlantic by way of a Dutch frigate, which landed in Virginia in August 1619, almost four hundred years ago. Africans were originally brought over as indentured servants and worked along with white indentured servants to resolve a labor shortage on the plantations. At the end of the time required to serve as an indentured servant, the African and other servants were freed from servitude and remained free. They were often given land.

But the labor market shortage continued as Africans and other servants were rotated from servitude to freedom. To tackle this shortage, the African servants who had not yet gained their freedom were recategorized as slaves for the "duration of their lives." Any new arrivals from Africa were immediately labeled as slaves. This occurred in 1691 about sixty-five years after the Africans originally brought here had already begun to receive their freedom. Again, those already freed remained free. This whole slavery thing was all about cheap and hard labor for the benefit of the few. Slavery played an extremely important role in the advancement of the southern plantation economy. Without the slaves, the South would not have survived.

Those who became slaves were emancipated just shy of 246 years later in 1865. There was a hundred-year period between 1676 and 1776 where slave activity was the most abundant.[80] Also, according to an article written on Virginia African Americans at FamilySearch. org, it is reported that Virginia had the largest number of free people of color in the United States since 1600 with probably 12-15 percent living as free inhabitants. In addition to being freed from indentured servitude, many of the free people of color were descended from the black slave men who had children by white indentured women, and as a result, these mixed descendants were manumitted or freed.

It goes without saying that African slaves were given new names or nicknames by their masters once they arrived in America making it impossible other than by DNA to trace the origin of ancestors who first arrived here. And once mixed, it seems impossible to trace most of the European or possible Indian ancestry as well without the same testing. As for the African ancestry, a majority of the slaves came from Nigeria, Senegal, and Gambia, and Ghana. Others came from Togo, Benin, Madagascar, and Mozambique. Those from Senegal and Gambia had a strong Muslim presence.[81]

African Americans from Virginia served on both sides of the Revolutionary War in search of freedom. Some African Americans were free before the civil war. There were fewer slaves in the area that seceded from Virginia and became West Virginia. West Virginia did not have many slaves since it was mainly a mountainous area and most of its land was located in the Appalachian Mountains. Slavery just was not profitable in this mountainous terrain. So those inhabitants who lived in that part of Virginia seceded in 1863. The few slaves that lived there were freed at that time and prior to the Emancipation Proclamation and others were already free.

Due to the loss of census data on and before 1830, many people are hard to trace before then. To add to this dilemma, so many people in the South carried identical names no matter what race, making it difficult to determine one person from the other. For instance I located a white William Hatcher and my second great-grandfather was a black or mulatto with the same name, and they both carried the same year of birth. Prior to the 1850 census, there was no designation of race, and I assumed I had stumbled upon my second great-grandfather's family when I located records for William Hatcher in the earlier databases. I was definitely wrong as pictures came to surface and none of the family looked anywhere close to being African American or even mixed. Also, that William Hatcher eventually moved to another state. I believe Kentucky or some other state to the west of Virginia. My second great-grandfather remained in Virginia and had not moved to that location. You will eventually know when you have made a wrong turn. The pieces just do not fit together.

Race was however specified in the 1850 census, making it easier to decipher which person belongs to which bloodline. The 1870 census was the first to contain the names and identities of slaves freed by the Emancipation Proclamation.

The Indians who were enslaved or who may have been free assimilated with the Africans in Virginia and West Virginia. They married and bore children and established communities and the Indians no longer distinguished themselves as Indians and no longer belonged to tribes. Their offspring took on mainly the African characteristics and the true Indian features began to fade to the point where the Indian characteristics were no longer discernible. Mixed people were labeled as black or mulatto as time progressed. In the beginning of the term mulatto in the colony of Virginia, the Virginia law clearly denoted a mulatto as a person with Indian and African mixture. Within time, those mixed with African and European blood were also identified as such.

A part of my paternal side started with the Hatcher and Odrick mulatto (mixed blood) families who were born in the northern part of the State of Virginia. My second great-grandfather William Hatcher Sr. was born in December 1846 in an unidentified county that seceded from Virginia in 1863. I have to assume that he may have lived in the northern panhandle or somewhere located close to Fairfax County. In the 1870 census, he is living in Fairfax County, Virginia, with his wife, my second great-grandmother, the former Sallie Odrick, and her family. Both second great-grandparents' parents, my third great-grandparents, were born in Virginia as well. Neither of them shows up in the census until 1870, which is an indication that both second great-grandparents were probably children of former slaves.

We know for sure that our third great-grandparents Alfred and Anna Maria Odrick and their families were former slaves because of their notoriety and recent historical markings and a park that was named in honor of second great-grandmother Sallie's father, my third great-grandfather Alfred Odrick, in Fairfax County, Virginia. I am not sure of the ethnicity in which they were mixed. I know that Hatcher is an English name meaning the "gate." I am having a hard time identifying the origin of the surname Odrick. It could have been a foreign word meaning carpenter. I do know that Fairfax County had a strong British presence. It was in fact a British colony. Other than that, little is known about the earlier ancestry for second great-grandfather William Hatcher and third great-grandparents Alfred and Anna Maria Odrick.

Pleasant Grove Methodist Episcopal Church was founded in 1895 and my second great-grandfather, William Hatcher, was one of the first seven trustees who had established this church. Records indicate that Pleasant Grove Methodist Episcopal Church was built and attended by African and Native Americans and there could have also been white Americans in the congregation as well. A book, *Images of America McLean*, written by Carole L. Herrick, contains information about my third great-grandfather Alfred Odrick and my second great-grandfather William Hatcher and, among other things, references the establishment of one of the first African American communities in Virginia, the historic Odrick's Corner.

Specifically, second great-grandfather William Hatcher was one of the seven trustees who formed the historic Pleasant Grove Methodist Episcopal Church in McLean, Virginia. The seven trustees were Samuel Sharper, John Willard, Elmead Sharper, William Sharper, William Hatcher, William Harris, and William Grayson.[82] As stated earlier, this church was formed by African and Native Americans. Samuel Sharper led the congregation. "How beautiful are the feet of those who preach the good news" (Romans 10:15). The congregation originally held its worship services at Odrick's Corner School until they acquired their own land and erected a building where they held their first service in 1896. This church still stands and is now a museum and it is designated as a historical site.

As a side note, research conducted by Paul Heinegg states that those with the surname Hatcher were free people who mixed with the Indians. Nevertheless, they may have also been slaves and prior to 1870 may have been identified on the slave schedule as merely a number or they could have been living among the Indians in the mountains of West Virginia. As in other places, we do know that those of other ancestry who mixed with the African produced children who looked black and after some time the Indian or white features were no longer there. I am unable to verify any information for my second great-grandfather to the third generation other than he was listed as both mulatto and black.

As a point of reference, in about 1705 the Powhatan Indians in Virginia were described as "almost wasted." At one time they had twelve villages, eight of which were on the Eastern shore, the only one of consequence being Pamunkey, with about 150 souls. Those on the Eastern shore remained until 1831, when the few surviving individuals, having become so much mixed with Negro blood as to be hardly distinguishable, were driven off during the excitement caused by the slave rising under Nat Turner.[83]

Eventually, Virginia passed stringent segregation laws in the early twentieth century and ultimately the Racial Integrity Act of 1924 mandated every person who had any African heritage be deemed black. Walter Plecker, the head of Vital Statistics office, directed all state and local registration offices to use only the terms "white" or "colored" to denote race on official documents and thereby eliminated all traceable records of Virginia Indians. All state documents, including birth certificates, death certificates, marriage licenses, tax forms and land deeds, thus bear no record of Virginia Indians.[84]

Second great-grandfather Hatcher was not originally from the Fairfax County area and in the 1870 census the assistant marshal noted that he was from West Virginia. The census does not state the specific county, but I assume it was a county that seceded from Virginia in about 1863 and was probably located in the panhandle region in the mountainous areas where the Native Americans were forced to live. I suspect he was from Jefferson County or some other neighboring county that contains the Blue Ridge Mountains and the Shenandoah River. But at the time of his birth, the area where he was born and raised was at that time the state of Virginia. Records indicate that he and his parents were born in the state of Virginia.

A treaty was formed with the Indians in northern Virginia that required them to remain west of the Blue Ridge Mountains and on the Maryland side of the Potomac. I know my ancestors were black, but there had to have been additional mixtures as we all know and in this case the ancestry was probably mixed with Native American. They may have also mixed with the white European. But like a lot of my ancestors, a more in-depth study would need to occur to go back that far and to identify even the African countries from where they originated let alone the European and/or the Indian heritage. This ancestry was so long ago and since then such blood has thinned in the descendants. So, without a doubt, we are African Americans and have been so for some time. I merely am trying to put together those who created us from the distant past, and I am not trying at all to water down my own self-identity as an African American.

Our Hatcher ancestors were Methodist Episcopalians and this included my father, his father and his grandfather and granduncles and at least one of his first cousins who lived in Waterbury, Connecticut. Others on my father's side were Episcopalians to include his mother, Romietta Jackson Hatcher, and his grandmother, Nettie Dubois Hatcher, who was his father's mother. Both lived in Connecticut. I now know that Methodist Episcopalian, Episcopalian, AME Zion, and Baptist were dominant among my people.

My mother's mother was Baptist and her brother attended the African Methodist Episcopalian Zion church. My mother joined the Mt. Olive AME Zion Church after we, her children, left home so that she could worship with my father who was of the Methodist Episcopalian denomination. In McLean, Virginia, the Hatcher ancestors attended Pleasant Grove Methodist Episcopal Church. The Odrick family appears to have been members of Shiloh Baptist Church. My cousin Dianne S. Hardison is still a member there.

I do know that a great majority of the white Hatcher plantations were located in the southern part of the state of Virginia and second great-grandfather William appears to be from the northern area. So I have to assume that either our ancient Hatcher ancestors choose that name but were not slaves belonging to the southern plantation owners, or one of the Hatcher ancestors may or may not have been fathered by one. All I know, the Hatchers were listed as mulatto and sometimes as black, and they originated from mixed people. I also know that the white Hatcher members were British and there is an abundance of white families mainly from southern Virginia with this surname. I have found no evidence that we are at all related.

I was able to locate a few African American families with the surname Hatcher listed in the 1870 census, when slaves had already been freed and who were located in the northern Virginia area. I know second great-grandfather William had not been alone and on his own. This didn't seem to be the norm during the time that he was born. Based on his determination and fondness for his family, he had to have had family. Again, I find several individuals who are mulatto or black who were born during the time of second great-grandfather's birth who could have been his siblings or other family members, but I have not been able to verify this. Since he had already left home by 1870, and there is no clear record before then, I just don't know which African American Hatcher family or families are related to us. I am still searching and hope to stumble upon some more definitive facts in the near future. Having located several families in the northern part of West Virginia with the surname Hatcher who are listed as black, either one or all could be a part of this seed.

My progenitors that I located in Virginia were definitely listed as mulatto. Virginia actually had laws on the books that clearly defined a mulatto. This law was used quite extensively to prosecute white women who had children by a slave of African descent. Mulatto was first defined in law as a child of an Indian and the child, grandchild, or great-grandchild, of a negro. In my estimation that means if you were mixed and had one-eighth black blood or more, you were mulatto. Some years later, the law further clarified its application of the law to those mixed with white blood. Translated this meant that every mixed person who had one-fourth or more of Negro blood was deemed a mulatto.[85] I think that means if at least one grandparent was black in spite of the other three grandparents being white the person was considered a mulatto. So a mulatto had to have had one grandparent who was white to be considered a mulatto, otherwise the person was listed as black. I know when I was growing up, if you had one ounce of black, you were black. Again, I am simply trying to decipher the intent of the law. After a while with all the mixing between black and white and Indian, the terminology mulatto was dropped.

The order in which these laws were established was interesting and leads me to the conclusion that Africans and Indians mixed and produced children prior to the Africans mixing with the whites. As I said earlier and throughout this writing, what was produced was an African American race and we are ultimately African American and our ancestors were of various races and nationalities over the years. The African gene was too strong to be much of anything else. I also want to point out that the Indians were the first to become slaves in spite of being the original inhabitants in this land. Therefore, Indian slavery is the original application of white superiority in America. The Europeans literally stole the Indian's land. Ironically and over time, both African Americans and Indians themselves became slave owners especially when they needed help on the land they had acquired.

Because so many of our ancestors located in records were noted as mulatto, there is a need to clarify and document this. This helps us get to the bottom of our roots at least to the African American bloodline for genealogical purposes. Mulatto served as an identifier and allowed for data to be collected on mixed-people who were born during a certain period of time at least in America. Taxes were determined and applied differently to mulattos and Indians than they were to whites and blacks. Also, the mixed child's status was determined based on whether the mother was white or black. Mulatto children birthed by a white woman were free, while a child birthed by an African woman and a white man was enslaved or served as an indentured servant.

The terminology mulatto also showed the process and the development of an African American race in America. It had its purpose during those times and definitely assisted me in search of my ancestors, derogatory or not. I will not however turn my head to its negative intent. A few whites were indeed the controlling force in this country, and they had their way even with their own people who often served as indentured servants.

The laws were numerous regarding the Negro, the mulatto, the Indians and the poor white. The laws seemed to be twisted and developed as needed to control those of different ethnicities or who had different status. The lawmakers must have driven themselves nuts keeping up with all this. So identifying the make-up of a mulatto is very complicated. We must also remember that a very small portion of white people were landowners and in control. All others worked for them in some form or fashion and only a small number were wealthy enough to own plantations and their own slaves and bondservants. But the few ruled this country and had given themselves the authority to make critical decisions.

The word mulatto originated from the Spanish or the Portuguese language and was meant to be derogatory just like the other names they called us and still call us today. The Spanish and Portuguese owned the boats that transported our ancestors from their homelands to America. These boat owners were treacherous, mean, and ungodly. Even so the meaning matters not to me at this point in time. But knowing the word's origin from the foreign word "moolay" meaning mule, it is not comforting to me. We, as a people, will not accept this terminology in the present or the future and probably would not have found it acceptable even yesterday.

In my opinion, name calling does not stop with "mulatto." I am not particularly fond of the word "Negro," which means "black" in Spanish and probably was also meant to be derogatory at that time superseded by the ridiculous label, "colored." Since the white slaveholders had superiority complexes, these titles could not have had any good purpose or intent.

Slavery should have never existed, but it did. All we can do is embrace our ancestors who had to move forward through such demoralizing times in hopes of providing a better life for the generations to follow. Therefore, any offensive terminology to describe us is simply dead. We will define ourselves as we stand with dignity and ancestral pride. I am proud to be an American, and I am more than proud to be an African American. I embrace my heritage.

Anyone defined as a mulatto was treated the same as a Negro, or an Indian. The laws clearly stated its application to the "Negro, mulatto and Indian." Some of these laws were basically the same as those used in other states. There is nothing new under the sun. Africans and Indians were disenfranchised. There had to be more suffering than not amid the devastating and demeaning institution of slavery and servitude and it was widespread. In spite of man's inhumanity toward man, many of our ancestors persevered with strength and dignity. Thank you, Jesus. I know what it feels like in these current days on a smaller scale, and I can only imagine what was endured then. It had to have been rough, and at the same time our ancestors had to have been tough.

Some slaves worked from sun up to sundown. The tasks of those in the field were planting and harvesting crops. Crops varied and so did the tasks. Cotton, sugar, tobacco, and rice were some of the most prevalent of the crops produced in the South. Servants lived and worked in the slave owner's house, which I am told is a whole different story. Some, like my third great-grandfather Alfred Odrick, had special skills. He was a carpenter. Other African Americans with skills during that time included coopers, boatmen, and blacksmiths. Third great-grandfather Alfred was not only a carpenter but he was also a farmer. As an artisan, he was much more valuable to his owner and was more than likely treated better than the others. The skill level of the slave determined the treatment of the slave by his or her owner.[86]

Slaves also drove carriages transporting the owner and his associates and family and others worked in hemp fields. It appears a number of slaves volunteered for this latter task.[87] I believe I know why. For those who cooked, the yard served as the kitchen. On some of the larger plantations, slave kitchens were built specifically for this purpose.

In all, I do believe that some of our very ancient ancestors were treated cruelly from one day to another, and they were subjected to hard labor. Again, to go over all the facts and occurrences regarding slavery in the South would take a book and so many books and stories have already been written.

Even if our ancestors were free, their tasks were the same: laborers, farmers and farmhands who tilled and built the undeveloped land or served in other ways as they worked toward acquiring, or had already acquired, their own land. Even if free, the real and only difference was that they were not listed as someone's property but they still did not have the same rights as the Europeans. Free or not they had a lot of children and a lot of mouths to feed. They survived in the mountainous areas and on the farmlands. They survived in the north and in the south. But what is disturbing is the number of children who could not fight off the diseases and died young and some upon birth or shortly thereafter. Some mothers died in childbirth. Life just was not easy though some indeed were blessed more than others. A prayer life was definitely in order, and I know they prayed, and they prayed, and they prayed quite often.

As much as that era will never sit right with me, I am proud of my ancestors and what they endured. They had to be exceptionally strong to survive such evilness and such self-serving and pompous individuals. This was a period of time when it was the master versus the servants who were black, Indian, and poor white.

Records indicate that indentured servants outnumbered African slaves throughout the seventeen and eighteenth centuries. No difference as they socialized together, farmed together and even produced babies together. I know those who are currently classified as white, and have a problem with those who are people of color, wish this was not a fact, but it is. Their ancestors were not the aristocrats that those of today thought they were. For most, their ancestors were merely servants and some of those servants produced children of color. Those in this country need to learn the truth about how this country actually came to be. Since there is so much written on slavery in the south, I strongly recommend that you surf the Internet and locate books on slavery and read what has already been so eloquently written about this institution. I can only summarize it and will do so in a few words. We were exploited.

The rest of this document will trace my people who were products of slavery in the South and their stories and their plights to freedom. What we do know is that our second and third great-grandparents in Virginia were identified as mulatto when the term was being used to distinguish mixed people from all others. Everything God made was beautiful! What we do know of both second great-grandparents is that they were mixed people of African descent, which must have begun when the roots of those before them were supplanted from across the water.

We also know that in Virginia the terminology mulatto was originally applied to the children of African and Indian ancestry. Sometime later when mixing occurred between white and black, the offspring from that mixing were tagged in the same way. Records indicate that at some point a lot of intermixing between black and white was occurring in Virginia though it has remained pretty hush-hush over the years. No matter what, when the time came to no longer identify and collect census data on mulattos or to tax them differently, these same ancestors were listed as Negro, colored or black. Few with mixed ancestry managed to pass as Indian or as white since a mixed-race African American child mainly resembled the African American parent and less the Indian or white parent. The African gene was so very strong and dominant though our shades of black began to vary. A few even managed to pass as white.

I may never know the full extent of my heritage as my ancestors traveled without a say from the coasts of Africa, from the islands of West Indies, and from other unknown places to this our newfound homeland. The fact is that their struggles, their labor and their pain allowed us and others before us to be free and this is of utmost importance to me. The Word says that the prayers of the righteous are heard, and they are answered. I know somebody prayed for me.

Very few of the offspring of our ancestors born in the South remained there after the late quarter of the 1800s and the early 1900s. Some didn't move very far, maybe seventeen or twenty miles away from their place of birth, and they settled in Washington DC. It is known that following the civil war, African Americans in the Washington DC area had the opportunity to earn money in those boom times. Job opportunities were available to children of former slaves and to those who labored and were born free. In Washington DC, domestic work was the most available means of employment for most of the African American females.

Some of my ancestors from the south went as far north as possible and that was to Connecticut, and they remained there. They mixed with and married those from the North and by the time I was born and knew them, they had already developed the Northern ways. I knew very little about the South and had not visited there when I was growing up.

In addition, a few in my Northern ancestry line had already moved further north to Vermont and Massachusetts and then there were those born and who resided in New York including one of my great-granduncles from Virginia as well as others. Others had settled in Philadelphia, Pennsylvania, Baltimore, Maryland, or as previously stated Washington DC as big cities began to blossom. Even Washington DC is considered more mid-Atlantic with a northern flavor, especially today, as it connects to the great Northern cities. It matters not that it is located below the Mason Dixon line. The Mason Dixon line originally served as a demarcation line among four US states, forming part of the borders of Pennsylvania, Maryland, Delaware, and West Virginia then part of Virginia. Things have since changed. The attitudes and mores are different today.

The rest of this story will deal with the plight and progress of my family. These ancestral stories may be of major interest to those who are a part of this family and know it and those who will be surprised to find that we are in fact related. Others may want to use this as a model for their own ancestral trail. I am looking for those who I do not know to come forward and identify themselves if they are part of my ancestry. I am open to learn more about our ancestry and to correct any information contained in this document and to add things that I was unable to uncover.

For those not related to me, I do hope that this document encourages you to research and locate your family and your ancestors and to undertake this wonderful and informative journey. What I like most about this document is that it is unedited and it tells the story based on raw footage and facts. I am more interested in getting the story out there without too much tampering from an unrelated and third party than being too overly concerned about finding one or two typos out of 68,554 words. However, I simply despise errors. But I can tell you that it is indeed hard to edit your own work for minor mishaps. If you decide to do the editing, which I do not recommend, expect to read your document over and over again and pray for the best. A document this extensive would never be finalized otherwise. Therefore, if you see any errors, just let me know since my goal is perfection. Amen.

Third Great-Grandparents Alfred and Anna Maria Odrick

My third great-grandfather Alfred Odrick was listed in the 1870 US census as a mulatto, which indicates that he was the product of mixed ancestry. His wife, my third great-grandmother, the former Anna Maria Riddle, was also listed as mulatto. They could have been children of white servant women and African fathers, or vice versa. They could have also been children of slave owners or one or more of their parents were. I really do not know. There was so much intermixing going on. I can't help but share a statement I found regarding the secret of interracial sex relationships in Virginia. It reads as follows: Interracial sex remained the worst kept secret in Virginia throughout the eighteenth century. "Despite the legal and moral prescriptions against it, sex between whites and blacks was indeed commonplace. White women and black men occasionally formed relationships. In fact, one historian has suggested that in the first part of the eighteenth century, white women bore more mulatto children than did black women."[88] This is another interesting finding as the lives of the white population and the black populations began to intertwine in various ways, and they even produced children together.

Third great-grandmother Anna Maria was formerly Anna Marie Riddle and like her husband was born a slave and also had mixed parentage. She reportedly belonged to the Todd family of the Difficult Run neighborhood in Fairfax, Virginia. Third great-grandfather Alfred belonged to the Coleman family. At this time, I am unable to trace either one of my third great-grandparents any further back in our ancestry. I don't know if they were one-half or one-fourth African American. All I know is that they were mulatto, and they were slaves. They were parents to second great-grandmother Sallie and her siblings and the children were classified as mulatto. As time passed the descendants were classified first as mulatto and eventually as black.

The plantation from which third great-grandfather was freed was owned by the white Coleman family in Dranesville, Virginia, now McLean, Virginia, headed by John Coleman who was supposedly killed by the Yankees in the civil war. John Coleman's death may have freed my third great-grandfather ahead of schedule but not much earlier than 1865. If he was freed early or manumitted, the law may have required him to move from the area where he was enslaved. This would explain his move to Chicago. Some descendants of John Coleman may still live in the Virginia area even today.

I do know that both Alfred and Anna Maria were freed blacks when the Emancipation Proclamation was passed and at the time of the 1870 census. Prior to that, third great-grandparents Alfred and Anna Maria Odrick moved to Chicago where he earned a living as a carpenter. They returned home to Virginia, and in 1872, third great-grandfather Alfred started an African American community referred to and recently marked as Odrick's Corner. Third great-grandfather Odrick also helped organize and probably helped build a one-room schoolhouse that was named Odrick Schoolhouse. It was built adjacent to his property and his home in 1879. The schoolhouse was eventually expanded. This schoolhouse was a multiuse facility as community meetings and church meetings and services, specifically Shiloh Baptist Church and then Pleasant Grove Methodist Episcopal Church, were held there.

Again, my second great-grandfather William Hatcher was one of the founding fathers and first trustees of Pleasant Grove Methodist Episcopal Church along with three members of the Sharper family, Samuel Sharper, Elmead Sharper, and William Sharper. The other three founding fathers were John Willard, William Harrison, and William Grayson. Both Shiloh Baptist Church and Pleasant Grove Methodist Episcopal

Church are designated as historic sites on Odrick's Corner in McLean, Virginia. The first pastor of Shiloh Baptist Church was Cyrus Carter whose son Andrew Carter married third great-grandfather Alfred's sister in-law who I assume to be third great-grandmother Anna Maria's sister.

The white people in this area referred to third great-grandfather Alfred as "Uncle Alfred." He was so much respected that even the family of his former slave owner, the Coleman family, attended his funeral when he died in or around 1893. Third great-grandmother Anna Maria died in 1907. In addition to the marker, the Alfred Odrick Homesite Park in Fairfax County was named and dedicated in 2010 to honor his accomplishments and to preserve these historical events.

As documented by the Thunderbird Archeological Associates, following the civil war, freed African American slaves in Northern Virginia purchased land, and they actually established communities in several locations within Fairfax County.[89] Odrick's Corner was one of them. The deed located in the Fairfax County Court and the Virginia Room of the Fairfax County Library records third great-grandfather Alfred's purchase of land and his settlement on Lewinsville Road. Odrick's Corner became a thriving neighborhood of African Americans after the civil war.

This area was a major battlefield during the civil war and my ancestors were witnesses to the battles between the Union and Confederate soldiers. They were probably witnesses to battles before then, probably as far back as the American Revolutionary War in the late seventeenth century and definitely during the War of 1812. This area was not far from the nation's capital and at least one president and first lady, President James and Dolley Madison, fled to this area for safety during the outbreak of the aforementioned war. The white plantation owners were very wealthy men and some were close friends to the presidents and their families and probably their staff.

Third great-grandfather Alfred devoted his life to improving the lives of African Americans in the McLean community, and he donated part of his land to the Odrick Corner's school. Unfortunately, it is hard to trace the Odrick family past third great-grandfather and my visit to Fairfax in search of more information about my unknown fourth great-grandparents was not successful. Unfortunately, Fairfax County has few records relating to enslaved persons prior to the Emancipation Proclamation. The records for those who were freed are scanty as well. However, I am fortunate to have the amount of information that has been collected by the library about Odrick's Corner.

I strongly recommend that you refer to the Internet under Alfred Odrick to read up on these historical moments and the numerous articles written. Some of these websites are included in the reference section of this document or can be located just by entering Alfred Odrick in Fairfax, Virginia, in the web address. This was a big accomplishment for the African American. My first cousin, three times removed, Ray Odrick Hatcher, would be so proud. It was Ray who kept these memories alive for those in the Hatcher family. He visited Odrick's Corner quite frequently where some ancestors still lived, and he would talk to us about this rich history that had not been fully uncovered and yet he knew it so well.

Other Odrick Descendants: Dianne Smith Hardison and her Family

I recently had the pleasure to meet one of my distant third cousins, Dianne Smith Hardison, who still lives in Great Falls, Virginia. She is also a descendant of Alfred and Ann Maria Odrick. We met for the first time on April 18, 2013, along with my husband and another of her distant cousins, my son, Watani A. Dubois Hatcher. Dianne was very much involved with the historic developments in recognition of our ancestor, Alfred Odrick. Alfred and Anna Maria Odrick were her second great-grandparents, and they were my third great-grandparents. Her great-grandfather was my second-great-grandmother Sallie Odrick Hatcher's brother, John. John was the second child born to Alfred and Anna Maria and Sallie was the oldest child. The meeting with Dianne was more emotional and heartwarming than I could have even imagined and we are now connected as family.

Dianne earned her doctorate in Human Resource Development from Virginia Polythenic Institute and State University. She is president and CEO of the Hardison Group, LLC, and she is Eastern area director of the Links, Incorporated. My sister Barbara and I had tried to locate Dianne a year ago. It wasn't until I visited the Shiloh Baptist Church and met and discussed my quest with its current pastor, the Reverend Dr. Robert F. Cheeks Jr., that I finally made contact with her. She called me that same evening and our family relationship took off from there. I am preparing her portion of my family tree and it is quite extensive.

As far as Dianne's immediate relatives who are descendants of the Odrick family, I found the following. Second great-granduncle John Odrick, son to third great-grandparents Alfred and Anna Maria Odrick, was married to Ellen Louise Odrick. From this union three daughters were born: Margaret Odrick, Edna E. Odrick, and Ethel Odrick. I also locate a granddaughter who is living with Ellen Odrick named Ada, and she is married to Joshua Mahoney. Second great-granduncle John must have passed at this time. I am not sure which one of her three daughters was the mother of Ada.

Dianne's grandmother was the former Edna E. Odrick who married Arthur Randall. They produced five children: Serena Randall, Edna Bernice Randall, Eloise Randall, Gloria Randall and Robert Randall. Dianne's mother was the late Eloise Randall Smith and her father was the late Covert Lamar Smith. Both of her parents are buried in Arlington Cemetery.

Her aunt Bernice Randall Payne had three children with two still living. Eric Randall is deceased, India Payne Bayton lives in Atlanta, Georgia, and Renee Serena Bernice Payne Ayala lives in Marlboro, Maryland. Diane also mentions another aunt Gloria Randall Martin who had a son Jon Martin, and they both are now deceased. These are some of the other descendants of Alfred and Anna Maria Odrick, and they are all my third cousins. I am just finding them, so there could be more information to come or there could be corrections.

I know there are more Odrick and Hatcher descendants, and I pray this writing will help me identify them. We know that Sallie Odrick Hatcher and John Odrick had four other siblings: Frank Odrick who married Martha Odrick. They remained in Virginia and may not have had children. Next in line is Thaddeus who I only locate in the 1870 census though I locate a younger Thaddeus Odrick in Philadelphia, Pennsylvania, and a marriage between Thaddeus Odrick and Alice Odrick who died in 1907. Lewis Odrick appeared to have lived his life as a single man. The youngest child, Anna Maria Odrick, named after her mother, married someone with the surname Washington. I am researching any information that may identify her husband and the names of any children they may have had and where they may have lived.

I do know that there were quite a few families with the surname Odrick living in Fairfax County, Virginia, and Washington DC. I located other Odrick family members in Philadelphia, Pennsylvania. I do hope more descendants come forward so I can determine who is who and how we are related.

Second Great-Grandparents William Hatcher and the Former Sallie Odrick

"Now the parable is this, the seed is the word of God" (Luke 8:11). Second great-grandfather William Hatcher (b. 1846) married the former Sallie Odrick, daughter of Alfred and Anna Marie Odrick. Third great-grandfather Alfred was a farmer and carpenter by trade and second great-grandfather William worked on his farm as a farmhand in 1870. As far as second great-grandmother Sallie Odrick Hatcher, she was most likely born into slavery in Dranesville, Fairfax, Virginia, in October 1852.

Second great-grandmother Sallie was the oldest child of third great-grandparents Alfred and Anna Maria Odrick. Second great-grandfather Alfred, a former slave, ended up owning his own farm and home and even built a school and an African American community in Fairfax County, Virginia. Census records reveal that this African American community included or was in close proximity to a number of white families.

Second great-grandparents William and Sallie married on December 22, 1869, in Washington DC. The 1870 census shows William working as a farmhand on his father-in-law's farm, and he is living with the Odrick family. Occupants of the household were second great-grandparents William and Sallie and her nucleus family as follows: her father and mother who were my third great-grandparents Alfred and Anna Maria Odrick, and Sallie's four brothers, John, Frank, Thaddeus, and Lewis. Second great-grandfather William was twenty-three years old and second great-grandmother Sallie was eighteen when they married. A younger daughter, Anna Maria, who was named after her mother, was born in 1871.

The 1900 US census indicates that second great-grandparents William and Sallie had had fourteen children with ten children living whose birthdates spanned a period of 1870 to 1893. The other four may have died in childbirth or shortly thereafter. This seemed to be a common occurrence in those days as sickness and disease ran rampant. Some mothers even died while birthing a child. Most of the ten surviving children born to second great-grandparents William and Sallie moved to Connecticut, New York, or Washington DC when they became of age or sometime thereafter.

The 1910 census data shows that second great-grandparents William Hatcher and Sallie Odrick Hatcher were living on their own property south of and adjacent to third great-grandparents Alfred and Anna Maria's farm, and they remained there. I was unable to locate markers for their graves in a couple of the graveyards I visited in Virginia. It is likely that they were buried on their own property. I did read an article indicating that my third great-grandfather Alfred was buried on his property, so other members of the family may be buried there as well in a private family cemetery on their own land. This was not unusual during those days. I found no record indicating that they had been reinterred, and I am not sure if there were once markers to indicate the spots in which they were buried. The only marker I found was for Alta Hatcher in Pleasant Grove's cemetery. She was born about 1907, and she died in the 1960s. I am not sure how she is related to us, and I have located no further information regarding her at this time. When I visit the Pleasant Grove museum, which was once the church, there could be additional information available for review. The museum was closed at the time of my first visit.

As stated earlier, William Hatcher (b. 1846) and Sallie Odrick Hatcher (b. 1852) lived in Providence, Fairfax, Virginia, and had fourteen children. This area originally designated as Providence has been renamed and has become a part of McLean, Fairfax County, Virginia. The children of my second great-grandparents were born in Virginia as well, and according to the 1900 US census, ten of the children survived. Once more, most of the ten children of second great-grandparents William and Sallie left the area when they became of age except for great-granduncle William Jr. who continued to live in McLean, Virginia, where I believe he died. It appears that the youngest daughter, great-grandaunt Ruth, also lived there for sometime before she moved to Washington DC.

Three of the older sons relocated to Waterbury, Connecticut, with one moving to New Rochelle, New York, after having lived in Waterbury, Connecticut, for some time. Conversely, the female offspring from William and Sallie moved to Washington DC, though I am not sure about their daughter Sallie or their son James, my great-grandaunt and great-granduncle respectively. I am unable to trace them any further by public record. My aunt Natalie and probably my father had the honor of meeting their great-aunts and great-uncles, but Aunt Natalie was not familiar at all with Sallie or James. She doesn't even recall hearing about them. So they must have passed before she was born or before she was old enough to know them.

Those who left the Virginia area were more than likely in search of better job opportunities and an overall better life. The developing city life had to be more attractive than farm life could ever be, and they probably had their parents' blessings to move forward, and like them, they followed their dreams.

Success was sure to come and a better life was guaranteed for the future generations of African Americans. The children to second great-grandparents William and Sallie were encouraged to focus on the future. They had to have been excited and like most of us when we turned into young adults, they were ready to venture out into the world or they stayed where they were and married.

Settling together most likely offered a sense of protection and family support. Anyway, the daughters were not far from home, maybe seventeen to twenty miles away. Even though Washington DC was very close to Fairfax County in Northern Virginia, travel may have been a little challenging during that time. Nevertheless, land and property records show that the Odrick family owned at least one horse and a wagon or carriage, so we know they traveled by horse and buggy and maybe sometimes simply by horseback. In 1910, a trolley line was built connecting McLean (Fairfax County) to Washington DC, and the village of McLean grew from this trolley stop in the middle of nowhere.[90] Fairfax County is now a part of the Washington metropolitan area. A major connection to the Washington DC Metrorail is currently under way and is close to completion. This area has definitely grown over the years and since the time that our ancestors first landed and were born there.

The Hatcher children's pattern of movement was typical as whole or partial families migrated together. One or two brothers probably moved and established themselves and sent back for the other brother as they reported that living up North was indeed better. They lived among other African Americans who had been born free, like them, and some whose family had not experienced slavery but may have also toiled in the fields or served in other capacities. Some of the Hatcher sisters voyaged to a common location in Washington DC though they did not travel that far to find their new home. They had to have been searching for job opportunities, a joyful life and a chance at city life as the doors of opportunity had begun to open. I now know that they were there with other relatives on the Odrick side to include their Uncle John and his wife, Ellen.

The Odrick-Hatcher Children Born to Second Great-Grandparents William and Sally

This section will start out with the oldest, great-grandfather Henry Hatcher and his wife, great-grandmother Nettie Dubois

Hatcher, and may divert to other thoughts and discussions before proceeding to the other nine children.

Great-Grandfather Henry A. Hatcher and the Former Nettie Dubois

Our great-grandfather Henry A. Hatcher was the oldest child in his family, and he was born in 1870. He married Nettie Dubois (b. 1871) who was the youngest child in her family. Both were listed as mulatto. They married in 1893 and lived in Waterbury, New Haven County, Connecticut. Their marriage ceremony took place at St. John's Episcopal Church, which is across from the Green in downtown Waterbury and in walking distance from their residence on Bishop Street and from 38 Bronson Street where they eventually lived. Based on her grandfather Alexander Dubois's religious affiliation as founder of St. Luke's Episcopal Church in New Haven, I am not surprised that the wedding was conducted in an Episcopal church even though great-grandfather Henry was raised as a Methodist Episcopalian. I am told there are similarities between the two denominations with a few slight differences

Like most areas of the country, travel in Connecticut was available by horse and buggy. We know from previous sections regarding my Dubois family that great-grandmother Nettie's parents, Henry A. and Sarah Brown Dubois, owned horses and carriages, and they were pretty well-off. Being rather classy and having the financial ability to do so, I know without a doubt that they traveled to their wedding ceremony in this latter mode. Unfortunately, her father, great-grandfather Henry Dubois, died a year before their marriage.

My great-grandparents and their children were the only African American (mulatto) family on the north side of the block in which they lived on Bronson Street. We grew up in the same home that they owned. The 1940 US census shows Nettie living among immigrants from Russia some who had relocated from New York and Pennsylvania. I actually remember one of the families and particularly the son Myron, whose parents were Russian immigrants, and who lived in the multiple family dwelling next to our home. Over time, others had immigrated from Poland, Lithuania, Austria, Hungary, Canada, Ireland, and Italy, to name a few. I actually had to teach an immigrant from Poland who lived next door to us in that family dwelling how to speak English. Her name was Charlotte, and she was Jewish. I enjoyed so much working with her when I was in the second or possibly the third grade. Because we had become close acquaintances, my teacher assigned me to work with her in class. She learned to speak the language well. I wonder where she is today.

My great-grandparents Henry and Nettie resided at 175 Bishop Street before moving to their permanent home at 38 Bronson Street. His birthday was November 29 and hers was September 28. Great-grandfather Henry died at the young age of fifty-two and great-grandmother Nettie passed at the age of eighty.

I remember some of our neighborhood families whose children I went to elementary school with and may have played with as well. In our earlier years, most of those in our neighborhood were white except for a couple of other families like the Wards and the Herberts. I remember when other African Americans began to move into this neighborhood and those we socialized with in high school as our borders and social sphere expanded and we became close friends to many more African Americans in the city. There were so many of us baby boomers during those times. It was exciting.

During my grammar school years we lived in a mixed neighborhood consisting of Jewish and Italian, a few Irish and a few African American families. After everyone was able to venture out, the neighborhood began to change and so did our friends. Even before then, the African American community had built the Pearl Street Neighborhood House years before, and it was later referred to as the Pearl Street Neighborhood Center. In the earlier years, this center was used as housing for the African American migrants from the South. In fact, I discovered that my great-grandmother Nettie also housed a number of those who had migrated from the south until they were able to support themselves, sometimes as many as five or six at a time. They appeared to be from one family who migrated to the north together.

However, during our development years, the neighborhood center gave African Americans throughout the larger community a place to send their children for cultural events. We gathered at the center for all kinds of events from my dance recitals as a child to Friday night dance parties when I became a teen. We learned to cook and sew there. We played basketball and ping-pong and cultural meetings were held there. The list of activities was rather long since it spanned many years.

My family never left this neighborhood over the years. But some of the children, like us, did. Our home had been my great-grandparents home and though my father was very successful, he refused to move even when the struggle to maintain the original middle-class character failed. Urban blight gradually took over and seemed to be hitting the larger cities in the State as well as other cities throughout the North.

Dad always stated that his roots were in this neighborhood and in this city, and he directed us not to disturb them or try to remove them even if he became ill. If we had tried to relocate him, which we did, we would not have been successful anyway. Dad did what Dad thought was best and we honor him. He was very good at determining what was right and in doing what was best for the family. But aging is aging and to change your surroundings at a later age can be difficult and oftentimes necessary, if you wish to extend your life. But Dad never moved from there. He had a lot of childhood memories in this place where his grandparents and his father had once lived and his roots in Connecticut indeed ran very deep. He ruled that neighborhood even when it became dangerous as he reminded even the crooks that his family dwelt there long before they did. The spirit had him protected and no one ever bothered him or his property.

Great-Grandfather Henry A. Hatcher, A Descendant of the Hatcher and Odrick Families

Great-grandfather Henry A. Hatcher steadily worked as a janitor, a laborer and a waiter. He was a waiter for the Women's Friendly League located at 29 Leavenworth, and he was also employed as a waiter at the Scovill House located at 293 North Main with his home at that time listed as 17 Hopkins Street. Scovill House was most assuredly named after the Scovill family who were very affluent and who owned and operated Scovill Manufacturing Company. Scovill was one of the largest employers of brass in this country for over one hundred years. Waterbury was once referred to as the Brass City and everyone owned something made of brass from buttons, to showerheads, from clocks, to lipstick holders, etc.[91] Scovill Manufacturing Company was also one of my father's first employers for a brief period of time. Other ancestors also worked and retired from there. However, it was not long after Dad's short employment with Scovill that he began a lifelong career and was the first African American professional employee for the State of Connecticut's Unemployment Compensation Office.

Waterbury at one time was a thriving city. Waterbury had the largest button industry and the largest clock factories in the world. In fact, Waterbury produced brass buttons for the federal uniforms during the civil war and made cartridge clips and other artillery during World War II making it a target for an outside bombing attack. The

Timex watch and the Mickey Mouse watches made Waterbury famous as well.[92] In the earlier years, travel was by horse and buggy and later by trolley and bus. It was a booming city with a lot going on from celebrities to tourism.

Emancipation in Connecticut occurred in the 1784 Connecticut laws, more than eighty-one years before the Emancipation Proclamation and before some of our northern ancestors arrived or had been born. Farms in the surrounding areas produced rye, Indian corn, onions, potatoes, apples, beef, hogs, cider, hay, oats, and buckwheat. Therefore the second, and even some third great-grandparents, born in the North had to have been born free in America and possibly others before them. Even so they also served and labored and owned their own land and had at least one grocery store. There wasn't much else to do. One thing was for sure, everyone needed to eat to survive. The population was small and the country was in the prime of its development. The elders from the North always stated to us that our ancestors were born free in the North and these words keep ringing in my ears.

Both great-grandfather Henry and his brother Joe worked at the Scovill House. One of the Scovill locations was listed as "Scovill House, Waterbury, Connecticut, CM Truman Hotel Company." Many businessmen from New York and other places visited this Waterbury city, and I would imagine they needed an upscale place to stay. Also, tourism was at an all time high as many people wanted to see this famous city. There may have been a couple of Scovill House locations since the places where my great-grandfather and my great-granduncle Joe worked showed different addresses. I know for sure that there was the Scovill Homestead located not far from where they lived.

Great-granduncle Joe had worked three or more jobs: as a waiter at the Scovill House at 114 Park Avenue, as a janitor at a place listed as Am. R. Co. at 156 Bishop Street, and as a barber at 30 Bronson Street. He lived at 156 Pearl and then at 60 Pearl Street. The homes that brothers Henry and Joe purchased were probably part of the property originally owned by the Scovill family. If not originally owned by the Scovill family, there was definitely other Scovill property surrounding that property at the time of purchase.

Being waiters at the Scovill Houses, which appeared to be guest houses and hotels and maybe even the private homestead, perhaps allowed them to rub elbows with the wealthiest businessmen coming in from New York, other surrounding towns and cities, and other places out of state. They obviously learned to invest in property and in land, and they followed the footsteps of their father William and their grandfather Alfred Odrick. Some heavy-duty dealings must have been occurring in those days. It pays to work hard and to know successful people.

Great-grandfather Henry and his brother, great-granduncle Joe, worked steadily and obviously did what they had to do. Hard work and dedication had resulted in very educated and successful children. Education was at the forefront and education was a must in the Hatcher, Odrick, and Dubois families and the other ancestral bloodlines as well. It started with third great-grandfather Alfred Odrick when he donated property and probably built one of the first schoolhouses for African American children in Fairfax, Virginia, in 1879, and perhaps he also helped construct a church or two. After all he was a carpenter by trade. Even before then, it started when third great-grandfather Alexander attended Cheshire's gentleman's school in the early 1800s. And there could be other such events to include the Jackson's attending one of the first schools for African Americans in New Haven, Connecticut, in 1811.

A spiritual life was also mandatory as evidenced by third great-grandfather Alexander Dubois being one of the founders of St. Luke's Episcopal Church in New Haven, Connecticut, on June 7, 1844, and third great-grandfather Alfred Odrick's connection to the building of Shiloh Baptist Church on Odrick's Corner in Fairfax, Virginia, in 1873. These both continue to be active and progressive African American churches today. In addition, second great-grandfather William Hatcher was one of the founding fathers and first seven trustees for the historic Pleasant Grove Methodist Episcopal Church located not far from Shiloh Baptist Church. Pleasant Grove is now a museum. This serves as evidence that education and a spiritual life were mandatory matters in our family since a couple of centuries ago.

Great-grandfather Henry Hatcher's employment helped him support his family and allowed him to provide a home for them at 38 Bronson Street. In 1910, the census listed him as a laborer living there. This home was actually built in 1900, prior to my great-grandfather purchasing this property outright via a quit-claim deed. He purchased this property on April 20, 1907, for one thousand twelve hundred dollars. Twelve hundred dollars in those days equates to sixty thousand dollars today. Land records indicate that it was purchased from David M. Cowles of Bethlehem. The estate of Cowles was being handled by his brother who lived in Pasadena, California. Based on property records, the Cowles were very wealthy and in today's terms would have been listed as millionaires.

Aside from that, great-grandfather Henry paid for this property in full and no mortgage was ever required or attached to this property still owned by my family today. The estate of great-grandfather Henry, dated June 13, 1923, passed this property to his family. Also, according to land records, great-grandfather Henry owned other property on French Street and Pearl Street that must have been sold upon his death. My mother, Viola Hatcher, recalls great-grandmother Nettie telling her how surprised she was to discover the amount of property owned by great-grandfather Henry shortly after his death. She had no idea that he had owned so much property to include a couple of homes in West Haven, Connecticut, close to Savin Rock. It appears that he was very adept and interested in real estate. I am not sure if Granddaddy inherited or owned his father's property at some point. I do know for sure that those other properties are no longer in the family today.

Prior to the purchase of their home, one of great-grandmother Nettie's nieces, Josephine, reportedly lived at 38 Bronson Street with her husband John Hale and their children. They may have rented the property from the Cowles family. Josephine and Alan divorced and Josephine and her children, Ruth, Alan, and Grace moved to Manhattan, New York. John moved to New Haven, Connecticut, where he attended the same church as my aunt Natalie, the former Natalie Roberta Hatcher. Aunt Natalie, my father's sister, recalls visiting and playing with Alan and Josephine's children. She thought Josephine was the sister to great-grandmother Nettie, but after searching through records, I found her to have been great-grandmother Nettie's niece. Josephine was the daughter to one of great-grandmother Nettie's sisters, Sarah Louise Dubois, whose married name was Ridley. Josephine was for that reason Aunt Natalie's cousin though their ages were years apart with Josephine being the oldest.

After great-grandfather Henry's death, records indicate that my great-grandmother Nettie continued to support the family by doing laundry at home and working as a waitress in a private school in Middlebury. All in all, great-granddaddy Henry A. Hatcher had secured a home for his family that was paid in full—a very wise move I must say. Progress was being made as more and more African Americans were becoming homeowners and landowners, including those on my mother's side. They were truly successful members of America's melting pot, and they lived a good and progressive life in Waterbury and in other places in New Haven County.

My great-aunt Virginia, my great-grandparent's only surviving daughter and the youngest child, died at the young age of thirty-eight from pneumonia. My aunt Natalie recalls that she had gotten caught in a thunderstorm and became quite ill and never recovered. Looking at the dates of death for many of my ancestors and the survival rate during childbirth, it is obvious that health care was a major issue during those times. The death of my great-aunt Virginia had to hurt great-grandmother Nettie who had already lost her husband and now her youngest child. I did not have the opportunity to meet her.

A tragedy of broken-heartedness from the loss of children and spouses continued to occur in this generation. Census records show that great-grandmother Nettie had had four births and two of those children lived, Granddaddy and his sister Virginia. Now, as a widowed parent, she was down to one, their son Theodore William Hatcher. But Granddaddy Theodore W. Hatcher had already left home to attend Yale, had married and had his own children and eventually moved to Philadelphia, Pennsylvania. Other Dubois family members were living and had lived in Philly as well.

One of great-grandmother Nettie's sisters, Mary Dubois Johnson, had also lost children due to early deaths. She had birthed fourteen children and was down to ten. Her sister, Sarah Louise Dubois Ridley, appeared to have also experienced the loss of her children. Records indicate and my cousin Asiila confirms the following, "There were epidemics of diphtheria that swept through the USA and Europe in the 1800s up through 1920 when the vaccine and *cleaner* water was made available to most people . . . babies often died from it. And the pollution was abysmal back then too—the beginning of the industrial revolution and factories everywhere. I looked up American Pin Company and got pages of all kinds of factories in Waterbury, Oakville, even. There was even an article bemoaning how bad the pollution was getting—"ruining the towns!" (Asiila)

African American Graduates of Old Yale - Granddaddy

My great-grandparents Henry and Nettie are recognized on Ancestry.com by the African American Graduates of Old Yale to honor their hard work, morals and belief that allowed their son, granddaddy Theodore William Hatcher, to matriculate and study at Yale, though he did not graduate. He is noted in the same manner on Ancestry.com as are other ancestors to include those from the Jackson seed. As I recently checked, more of our family members are being included as descendants of those connected to Yale for either their work or their education during these earlier days.

Instead of completing his education at Yale where he appeared to have been a student for at least two years, Grandfather Hatcher (Granddaddy) found a beautiful wife who served as one of the first African American employees for Yale, my grandmother Romietta Jackson, with whom he started a family. She was a secretary there. Granddaddy and Grandma Ro, as we called them, produced my aunt Natalie Roberta Hatcher and my late father Theodore William Hatcher Jr. Both children were born in New Haven. Without God, Jesus, the Holy Spirit and my ancestors, I would not be here today and know what I know. So I honor them and hold great admiration, respect and love for them.

Following are my great-grandparents Henry and Nettie's children who were born in Waterbury, Connecticut, and lived into adulthood: Theodore W. Hatcher (b. 1895) and Virginia O. Hatcher (b. 1903). Granddaddy's exact birth date was May 23, 1895. Both siblings were listed as mulatto when it was necessary to distinguish and enumerate those with mixed blood, which possibly started from a generation or two back. Their race was changed to black or Negro when the term mulatto was in the process of being or had already been phased out.

Great-Granduncle Joseph E. Hatcher

Joseph E. Hatcher (b. 1877) married Henrietta Marlow (b. 1880) and they lived in Waterbury, Connecticut, at 60 Pearl Street. Great-granduncle (Uncle Joe) and his wife (Aunt Hennie) were also listed as mulatto and then black or Negro in the subsequent census databases. Aunt Hennie, the former Henrietta Marlow, was born in Washington DC to Charles and Laura Marlow who were born there as well. They lived in the Georgetown area where Aunt Hennie's father worked as a laborer. Aunt Hennie's four grandparents were born in Maryland.

Aunt Natalie adds in a letter to me dated October 8, 2007, that she knew Aunt Hennie's sister who lived in New Haven. "They all liked to have a good time," she writes. I assume this was probably during the Roaring Twenties and/or the Harlem Renaissance or shortly thereafter when they were having their private moments and were letting their hair down. The Harlem Renaissance was one of the most influential and interesting periods of black history. Musicians, artists, photographers, poets, writers, and singers cropped up in Harlem. Fine clubs, fine clothes and fine cars! Let the good times roll. Langston Hughes was one of those celebrated. These were the times when our ancestors could actually celebrate the accomplishments of black folks.

Great-granduncle Joe held a high position as Most Worshipful Past Grand Master of the Prince Hall Masonic Lodge first from 1912 to 1914 and then in 1922. Great-granduncle Joe eventually introduced my father to the organization and encouraged him to become a member. Years later, my father also served as Most Worshipful Past Grand Master of the Prince Hall Masonic Lodge. Great-granduncle Joseph's son Edward was involved in this fraternal organization as well.

Great-granduncle Joe and his wife, Hennie, had five children and the two who survived were Edward Hatcher (b. 1904) and Raymond Odrick Hatcher (b. 1908). Edward married Edythe Booth and Raymond married Mary Alice who we called May. May was born in Alabama in 1910, and she had moved to New York. Raymond, whose full name was Raymond Odrick Hatcher, is author of Urban Renewal as a Catalyst, Wayne State University, Department of Public Administration, 1961, and he was an alumnus of Lincoln University. His graduate studies were held at Pendle Hill School in Pennsylvania and Wayne State University in Detroit, Michigan, where he received his master's degree in public administration. He had worked as assistant director of the Urban League in Detroit, Michigan, and had a number of years as director of several government organizations for housing and other social welfare agencies in Detroit and Philly. He also participated in an oral interview with Wayne State University in 1970 along with thirty-one other African Americans who played a role in trade-unionism in the United States.

Both of great-granduncle Joe's children were born in Waterbury, Connecticut. Edward was a member of St. John's Episcopal Church in Waterbury and Ray was a member of Mt. Olive AME Zion. Raymond was married for many years to Mary (May) Hatcher whom he had probably met in New York where she was living at the time. They lived a long life together and resided in Minneapolis, Minnesota, where they both expired. They always exhibited so much love. As far as I know, Edward or Ray had no living children.

The remaining siblings to brothers Henry and Joseph are as follows:

William Hatcher Jr. (b. 1879), the third child to second great-grandparents William and Sallie, lived in McLean, Virginia. He was married to Mary E. Hatcher (b. 1863), and he was self-employed as a farmer in the trucking farm business. They may have had children who I have not confirmed as their children at this time.

Janie Hatcher (b. 1882) moved to Washington DC. Aunt Natalie remembers her as one of the great-aunts visited and describes her as very beautiful and jazzy. I haven't been able to find much else about her through public records.

Daniel Hatcher (b. 1884) first moved to Waterbury, Connecticut, and he lived at 156 and then 263 Bishop Street. He later moved to 13 Hopkins Street. He appears to have moved to Waterbury in 1903 at the age of nineteen and relocated to New Rochelle, New York, in 1908. He was listed at one time as a porter, and he may have had other occupations after or before that. He married an immigrant named Bertha (b. 1883) in about 1905 or 1906 while they both were living in Waterbury. Bertha was born in Bermuda as was her mother. Her father was born in England and appeared to be white since she was clearly listed as a mulatto. At one point the census shows her from Bermuda, Ireland, instead of Bermuda Islands. The handwriting of the assistant marshals was sometimes slightly illegible causing misinterpretation of records by the current interpreters of the census. But it is definitely confirmed that she was from the island of Bermuda.

In summary, Bertha, a mulatto, immigrated to the United States in 1889 at the age of nine. She and great-granduncle Dan married more than ten years later. They moved to New Rochelle, New York, in about 1905 where they spent their lives. All of Daniel's family members are listed on the census as mulatto. His oldest son Raymond was born in Waterbury, Connecticut, and his other children in New Rochelle, New York. Their children were Raymond Hatcher (b. 1906), Inez Hatcher (b. 1908), Eleanor Hatcher (b. 1910) who appeared to have died in her first years, Dorothy Hatcher (b. 1911) and Everett Hatcher (b. 1912).

Cornelia Hatcher (b. 1887) married James Blackwell and records show them living at 336A M Place SW, Washington DC. Her children were Mary V. Blackwell (b. 1928) and Gladys Blackwell (b. 1930).

Sallie Hatcher (b. 1888) who was named after her mother has only been identifiable in the 1890 census. I have been unable to identify or locate her further in public records, and I do believe she may have passed at an early age.

Ada Hatcher (b. 1891) lived in Washington DC and was listed in her nephew Edward's 1937 obituary as Miss Ada Hatcher of Washington DC. In 1940, she is listed as married with the name Ada Henderson. Her husband is not identified but she is living with her sister Ruth at Ruth's residence. They both show employment as servants in a private home. I am told by Aunt Natalie that she had mobility problems and was confined to a wheelchair.

James Hatcher (b. 1892) is located on record only when living with his family as a child. It is difficult to verify where he lived in his adult life since several African American persons from the State of Virginia shared this name or he may have passed away in those earlier years.

Ruth Hatcher (b. 1893, d. July 1974) lived at 1768 U Street NW in Washington DC and married Opy Lewis Holland (b. 1888) who was from Fairfax County, Virginia, as well. Their daughter was Nellie M. Holland (b. 1908). Great-grandaunt Ruth lived in McLean, Virginia, and may have married there before moving to Washington DC with her husband in 1900. In 1910 they are living again in Fairfax County. The 1927 telephone directory shows great-grandaunt Ruth widowed and living at 1425 T Street NW no. 204 in DC. She worked as a cook. I find her living in both Virginia and DC from time to time. In 1940 she returns to Washington DC where she lived with her sister and her daughter on U Street where I visited her. It is here that she passed.

Great-granduncle Joe and his wife, Aunt Hennie, are most familiar to me since they lived up the street from us on Pearl Street before being called home to the Lord. I also was quite familiar with their son, Raymond Odrick Hatcher, in his later years. Ray and my father were first cousins one time removed, and they were extremely close. I remember our interactions as though it was yesterday.

One particular time, we had dinner together at a restaurant in DC. In attendance were my mother and father, my sister Barbara, and Ray and his beautiful wife, May. My sister Barbara and I resided in Washington DC after we both graduated from college. My sister Barbara had graduated from the University of Connecticut at Storrs, and I had graduated from Howard University in Washington DC. I remained in DC after graduating from Howard University. My sister had moved to DC during my senior year in college. My parents at this particular time were visiting. It was at this dinner that Ray spoke with excitement about Odrick's Corner, and he wanted us to get involved. My sister kept track of Odrick's Corner for many years. I was trying to locate our relationship to W. E. B. Du Bois.

Odrick's Corner

"If they obey and serve him, they shall spend their days in prosperity, and their years in pleasure" (Job 36:11). Raymond Odrick Hatcher talked extensively about Odrick's Corner, a place he visited quite often and whose label he carried throughout life having been given the middle name Odrick. During his childhood years, he spent time on his grandparents William and Sallie's farm, the Hatcher property located just south of the Odrick property located at Odrick's Corner. However, it appears that his grandfather had already passed when he was born and his grandmother may have passed when he was one. But other family still lived there, specifically Uncle Will Hatcher and Aunt Ruth Hatcher Holland. He was very close to his aunts and uncles. He may have spent time on his great-grandparents property as well though they may have also passed by the time he was born. I do know he visited this area from time to time and it seems as though it may have been annually. Census records show there was no mortgage on either property, and therefore, both had been paid in full.

Ray and my father were very close and it was Ray's efforts as an alumnus of Lincoln University that assisted my father in being accepted at Lincoln along with my father's exceptional intellect and his outstanding talents. My sister Barbara Hatcher stayed in communications with cousin Ray, and he provided her detailed information about Odrick's Corner in northern Virginia and a picture of him leaning on a sign with an inscription, Hatcher's Run. My grandfather Hatcher (Granddaddy) had also informed us of the sale of his grandparent's property on what had become the Dulles Access Road. We knew this, but didn't really pursue the matter since the property had left the family's possession. But my sister kept her eye on this since cousin Ray talked about its unique status as one of the first African American communities in Northern Virginia. When it was finally dedicated as such, my sister simply said, "Ray told us so."

Alfred Odrick (b. 1821) and Anna Maria Odrick (b. 1827) were the parents to Sallie Odrick (b. 1852) and her four brothers John Odrick (b. 1854), Frank Odrick (b. 1858), Thaddeus Odrick (b. 1866) and Lewis Odrick (b. 1868). Another daughter, Anna Maria Odrick was born in 1871. Third great-grandfather Alfred was a freedman, and he was a carpenter who established a one-room school, which was later expanded and built his own house after being freed and upon returning to Virginia. The 1870 census additionally records the fact that third great-grandfather was a farmer living in Providence, Fairfax, Virginia, which is the exact same area now known as McLean, and he owned land valued at $750.00. In today's dollar the worth of that property would have been $13,417.22. Though it was vast, most of his property was undeveloped land.

Horseback and horse and buggy were the modes of transportation during those days. In Northern Virginia, pine trees were plentiful and homes were being built by slave labor. This explains third great-grandfather Alfred's skills as a successful carpenter. Appearing in a Washington Star article dated June 9, 1918, is the fact that chestnut trees surrounded this land. Author and journalist John Harry Shannon (a.k.a. "the Rambler") refers to third great-grandfather Alfred as "a celebrated carpenter and house builder in those parts."[93] This article further states that the property purchased was part of the George West Gunnel farm where third great-grandfather Alfred built a log cabin and eventually upgraded the property to a house. The journalist wrote, "When the house was in its prime it was one of the best in that part of Virginia." He also reports that all the white people called third great-grandfather Alfred "Uncle Alfred."

But the story does not stop here as I comb through the historical and archeological research documents so graciously sent to me by the Commonwealth of Virginia. The researchers had a hard time piecing together that Sallie Hatcher was the oldest daughter married to William Hatcher and that Sallie was the former Sallie Odrick who was living at home in 1870. Marriage documents have been found that clearly show her maiden name. She was referred to in her mother's will as Sarah, which could have been her middle name. If I did not know what I know, this oversight would not have been corrected and we as descendants would have been excluded from these important accomplishments and the historical recognition of our ancestors. One thing that caused this omission was that the last name of the Odrick family was translated incorrectly in the 1870 census and has since been corrected by me from Odril to Odrick giving correct access to this bloodline. This incorrect information popped up when the 1870 census for William Hatcher was located. I can tell you that missing information caused by the illegible handwriting of the enumerators during that time makes it difficult to complete one's story. But when you know that you know and what you know, you will eventually get there. Just make sure you correct the information on Ancestry.com for the ease of other family members who are in search of their people.

Through oral history, I was aware that the Hatcher family owned property on Odrick Corner and that mother and father Odrick were grandparents to the Hatcher children. Without this piece of important information, I would not have been able to find this family connection for verification purposes. If others had had this knowledge there would have been an accurate connection of second great-grandparents William and Sallie not only to Odrick's Corner but to third great-grandparents Alfred and Anna Marie Odrick. I cannot stress enough the importance of gathering information from the elders who are still alive.

As far as Odrick's Corner, I would be remiss if I did not give credit and thanks to those in Fairfax County, Virginia, who sifted through many old records and produced a record that has made research regarding my Odrick ancestry readily available. Everyone involved did a wonderful job not having the advantage of the full oral history and facts that my family had obtained over the years. I also thank those who were forces behind identifying these historical accomplishments to include Dianne S. Hardison, one of the Odrick descendants, who I have finally had the pleasure to meet. She is a dynamic cousin who has received her doctorate in Human Resource Development and is Area Director for the Links, Inc., a national organization for accomplished African American women. I thank the Fairfax County Parks and Recreation, the Honorable John Foust, Dranesville district supervisor, and Jane Edmondson, Lewinsville Coalition president, for their personal assistance to me. I thank all others who participated in ensuring that Odrick's Corner was designated a place of historic interest.

Odrick Children

Third great-grandparents Alfred and Anna Maria's son, my second great-granduncle Frank Odrick was married to Martha Odrick who was born in 1869. According to the 1910 US census, Frank's brothers, my second great-granduncles, Lewis and John, were in the same household still living on the Odrick farm. Their brother Thaddeus is not listed and may have moved to Pennsylvania or he may have passed by then accounting for his absence from his mother's will. At the same time, second great-grandparents William and Sallie Hatcher are living on their own property south of the farm. The Odrick name is rather unusual, yet there are many records for mulatto or African American people with the last name Odrick from Providence, Fairfax, Virginia, and other places to include Washington DC and Philadelphia, Pennsylvania. I am sure they are somehow related.

Some of those that I located included Kate L. Odrick born January 1814 in Virginia and living in Providence, Fairfax, Virginia. She could be a sister-in-law to Alfred. Records indicate that she has a daughter named Annie Odrick (b. 1833). Annie had fourteen children with three living, and she was widowed in 1900. Martha Odrick (b. 1821) more than likely was also related to the family. There are other persons with the surname Odrick who were born between 1869 and 1893. Some are listed in the census with their spouses and could be the children of Alfred's siblings or grandchildren to one of his four sons or they are otherwise related. I am finding more definitive information as I meet other descendants.

Commonwealth of Virginia

Again, the research on third great-grandfather Alfred Odrick was pretty much completed at the direction of the Commonwealth of Virginia. I give special thanks to Fairfax County and all other associates who designated the place in which third great-grandfather Alfred dwelt an historic site and the Fairfax County Park Authority for naming a park in his honor. I also am grateful that the Pleasant Grove Methodist Episcopal Church has been designated a historic place. This is the place where second great-grandfather William Hatcher became one of the first seven trustees and more likely than not helped found this church.

Again, the information collected is stellar, though requiring one key correction and that is the fact that Sallie Hatcher was the oldest child and first daughter to Alfred and Anna Maria Odrick. There was mention in the documents provided that William Hatcher's wife was a daughter to Alfred and Anna Marie Odrick, but no validation had been documented until recently. After having informed the Commonwealth of Virginia of this, they have properly placed us on record as descendants. Again, it should be noted in third great-grandmother Anna Maria's will that Sallie's name is listed as Sarah, which was more than likely her middle name. It was not uncommon for our ancestors to use their middle names and interchange from first to middle name from time to time.

The Hatcher Property on Odrick's Corner

Sallie Odrick married William Hatcher on December 22, 1869, and the 1870 census indicates that her father, Alfred Odrick, owned seven hundred and fifty dollars worth of property at that time. Again, there are plenty of documents available to verify this. As I stated earlier, there are revelations along the way in the field of genealogy, even for those of us who are self-taught. The research conducted by the Commonwealth of Virginia tells the story much better than I can and their research closed several loops for me. In the process, and as noted earlier, articles regarding the dedication of Odrick's Corner allowed me to locate another one of the descendants, my third cousin Dianne Smith Hardison. Again, I had the honor to meet Dianne as we connected so easily as family. Newspaper articles record her involvement in the Odrick research and recognition. Her name and her photograph appear in a couple of the articles. She continues to live in the Fairfax County area in Great Falls, Virginia.

A picture of third great-grandfather Alfred's home was preserved by the Martin Luther King Library as well as an article written in "the Rambler" Sunday Star, a newspaper in Washington DC where pictures of the home and of the school are also printed. A copy of a deed, made on March 29, 1906, between third great-grandmother Anna Maria Odrick and three of her sons and her youngest daughter Anna Maria Washington has also been provided to us. This deed clearly indicates "the line of Hatcher" as one of the boundary lines for the property contained in the deed and it reads as follows: "thence southerly with said easterly side, the line of Hine, to the line of Hatcher; thence easterly with Hatcher to the westerly side of the Odrick's Corner road, etc." It is obvious that the older daughter Salle and her husband, William, my second great-grandparents, had been given a share of the family property earlier on or as a farmhand he had purchased this property from his father-in-law. Specifically, the properties owned by the Hatcher family as well as the Odrick family had no mortgages, and they were owned outright.

The deed mentioned above indicates that the Odrick property consisted of 8.5 acres. That is a considerable piece of land that equates to 370,260 square feet and quite a bit of it was undeveloped. Third great-grandfather Alfred Odrick recorded his will in October of 1894 with his wife being named as benefactor of his entire property. Third great-grandfather Alfred may have passed shortly thereafter.

As indicated earlier, my second great-grandparents William Hatcher and Sallie Odrick Hatcher owned and lived on their property adjacent to the Odrick farm. To the best of my knowledge and without much doubt, they did not move from Odrick's Corner and lived there until they passed on to the Lord. Odrick's Corner was their home. This property is land that Raymond Odrick Hatcher stated belonged to the Hatcher children. I do know that all the children had moved from the area and most had their own property and lived in Connecticut, Washington DC or New York. The surviving heirs at that time were not interested as Raymond Odrick Hatcher had often stated. Ray was concerned about this loss but could do nothing about it. I have not located a record of sale, but I hope it was sold and not taken because of lack of interest.

As a very young child Ray more than likely visited at least his grandmother and his uncle and aunt on this land. I do know that he continued to visit Odrick's Corner when he was older. Out of respect to Ray and his tenacity, let us not forget this important fact as part of the Hatcher genealogy.

North Carolina

Brief History of Slavery in North Carolina

The most impressive description of slavery in North Carolina was summarized by a professor at the University of North Carolina at Chapel Hill, Dana Durbin Gleaves, in an article I located and which is entitled "Slavery Across North Carolina." As a side note, my sister, Dr. Barbara J. Hatcher, earned her master's degree in public health at the University of North Carolina at Chapel Hill. Many of my ancestors were from Guilford County where Greensboro is the seat of that county.

Professor Gleaves states that slavery in and across North Carolina was diverse with many slaves working on small farms. She further states, "Others labored as skilled artisans, performed domestic work, worked in the shipping industry near the coast, or were able to "hire out" their time and worked for themselves."[94] I am elated to start out with this information and a quotation from this invaluable work, because it very well describes my ancestors from North Carolina, the Moore and Jones families.

For starters, my grandmother came from a family of more than seventy children in one generation whose births ranged from 1862 to 1903. The Moore family members were owners of a lot of farmland, and they themselves were farmers. Writing about my grandmother's thirty or more siblings and more than forty of her first cousins would take a book. I may decide to write separately about this phenomenon one day. What is important is that this is the maternal side of my family. There are relatives that I have never met. Most of us do not know each other or even know that each other exists. We are scattered across quite a few locations, but mainly on the East Coast and a large number of descendants by our great-grandfather's first wife, Flora Cardwell Moore, may still live in North Carolina. A few descendants from my great-grandmother Adaline Moore, the second wife to great-grandfather Thomas Moore, may continue to live in North Carolina as well.

The Moore Family

"But they that wait upon the Lord shall renew their strength" (Isaiah 40:31). My mother's family was a major part of our growing up since a number of them to include her mother, her brothers and her aunts and uncles and their spouses and children lived with us in Waterbury, Connecticut. The core of our developing years and the epitome of love, my grandmother Fannie (Nana) lived down the street from us on 18 Pearl Street with her second husband, Charles Cross, also originally from North Carolina.

In or around 1920, my maternal grandparents, Joseph Allen Jones and Fannie Moore Jones moved from Greensboro, North Carolina, to Baltimore, Maryland, with their two children. There had been four births prior to the move and two children survived. We called our grandmother, Nana. It was in Baltimore, Maryland, that their daughter, my mother, was born. We never had the opportunity to know our grandfather because of his early death. My mother does not remember much about him since he died when she was two years old. But Mom recalls that he was affectionately referred to by Nana as Allen. Shortly after Grandfather Allen's abrupt death, Nana moved with her children to Waterbury, Connecticut. Some of her sisters appear to have already relocated to Waterbury from North Carolina. My mother's brothers were Oliver Allen Jones (b. 1908) and Joseph Jones Jr. (b. 1911). They and many ancestors before them were born and raised in North Carolina.

Like other states, North Carolina was at one time heavily populated with slaves. But it was here that a portion of the Underground Railroad began to form, years before my grandparents and a few of my greats were even born. Between the late 1790s and 1820, a majority of the white residents in North Carolina had no wealth and often worked side by side with the African Americans and even owned farmland on the adjacent land. Many of the black and white people were neighbors and depended on each other to survive, and they even socialized together. These neighbors, particularly in Randolph and Guilford County, were antislavery, and they urged people to free their slaves. They assisted with the Great Escape to the North by way of the Underground Railroad, which was a network of secret routes and safe houses used to move slaves to free states and to Canada. The abolitionists and the Quakers were at the forefront of this movement.

The Underground Railroad actuality consisted of a vast network of people, both black and white, who greatly opposed the exceptionally cruel and demeaning institution of slavery that only really benefitted the wealthy. By way of this escape route, slaves would find shelter, food, and protection in these safe houses often referred to as depots. They were moved from one location to another until they reached their freedom. Some died en route. Others survived. During a four-year period, a hundred thousands of slaves escaped using this method.

Unlike many other freed blacks in North Carolina, Nana's family appeared to have been from freed bondservants, and they owned plenty of farmland. It is confirmed by relatives still living that they owned very large farms. In 1870, they are listed as free inhabitants.

Paul Heinegg's writing, "Introduction to Free African Americans from North Carolina and Virginia" traces the Moore bloodline from 1665 to about 1776 through court records and dockets. Records from court proceedings include such things as being sued by the white man for slander or debt, to producing a master for their children in order that they may be bound out as the law directs. Other proceedings involved the buying and selling of land, the recording of birth, death and marriage documents, as well as a petition for one of the younger Moore adults to be released from bondage or service having reached the age of twenty-one. It appears that the court ruled in favor of the Moore family in many of the court cases.

The majority of the Moore family appears to have been free or indentured, and they produced quite a few children to say the least. According to Paul Heinegg, in the early beginnings they themselves owned slaves and had to ask the court to liberate any black children born to slave women based on their status as unmarried and free. They were often in the court minutes and dockets referred to as "free negroe" or "free colored" and listed as a servant with a further clarification written as "but not a slave." There was clearly a difference. They were also referred to as the "free Moore family" or by their full name such as "Abraham Moore a free negroe" or "Abraham ye Negro at Mr. Allen's quarter" (tithable). The terms "taxable" or "tithable" indicted freedom.[95] Even though I am offended by these denigrating references to our people, these things are only included as emphasis and to exhibit the white man's disrespect for our people, free or not, indentured or slave.

The Moore family married slaves and former slaves and produced children. They were taxable or tithable in their own households as early as 1665, almost 350 years ago, and throughout court records dating back to 1776. What happened before 1665, I do not know for sure. But I do know that Africans and other people were indentured and not slaves prior to 1691. Their original status as indentured servants explains the free status of the Moore family since they may have served their time as indentured people before then, and they may have already been freed by the applicable laws.

Without some sort of descriptive labels, it would have been impossible to separate whites from blacks and this would have made it difficult for me to trace my bloodline or to feel how they were treated in spite of obtaining freedom. Remember, racial identifiers were not included until about the 1850 census, but name calling had occurred for some time. As I stated earlier, in these brand-new days, we will choose what name is attached to our race and ensure it is done with extreme dignity and respect toward our people. Still, the battle for this continues even today as we continue to be referred to by appalling names by those who obviously did not and do not believe in Jesus. If some of these same despising people search their genealogy, they may be shocked to find that they too have African ancestry.

The Moore family sometimes purchased property in hundreds of acres, and they also sold land. They were in essence real estate agents buying and selling property. They appear to have been more bondservants than slaves. Some of the more ancient ancestors probably lived and owned property on the eastern shores of North Carolina where the slave ships landed close to Beaufort County, and they moved to other counties as they gained their freedom. The more recent ancestors were born or they lived in Rockingham, Guilford, and Franklin counties in such cities or towns as New Bethel, Greensboro, Huntsville, and Cypress Creek.

I find Paul Heinegg's research regarding the African Americans with the surname Moore quite interesting. Heinegg's research starts with Abraham Moore born in 1665 and basically ends with "Old Punch and Rachel Moore" and Keziah Moore a "real estate agent" in Beaufort County. There were a number of African Americans with the surname Moore in Beaufort County who were free from as early as 1685. They owned quite a bit of land, and this land was often adjacent to land owned by whites.

This has been the pleasant side of that period for the Moore ancestry. We know they suffered somehow throughout their lives in North Carolina. Severe pain was endured during this period by many people of color, free or not. I know there were many different stories for matters not recorded and that were handled out of court. After all, slavery and servitude had its purpose, and that was cheap labor to increase the wealth and standing of the few white wealthy families. Not much has changed today.

The bottom line is that African Americans were imported to this country to provide free labor on the plantations while only a few white men got rich. As we know, the Indian slaves were already inhabitants of this land. I do know that black and white people in North Carolina had farmland in close proximity to each other. The main goal no matter what race or ethnicity was to feed and raise their families. They too may have come from families who were indentured servants and had been freed when their time expired, and they were given land as was required by law.

Living in proximity on farms supports the fact that not many of the white people were wealthy, and they had to farm just like us to survive. Because they worked and lived so close to each other, a majority of the white population supported freedom for the African American, and they assisted with establishing the beginning of the Underground Railroad.

I am told by one of my elders Margaret Moore that these writings about the Moore heritage are about my family and their ancient ancestors in North Carolina over three hundred years ago. Abraham Moore who was born 1665 may have been one of the first of the Moore clan to land in North Carolina.[96] Some or at least one of the Moore slaves may have originated or had been captured from the island of Barbados.

I give total credit to Paul Heinegg for this extensive research. Again, Heinegg's "Introduction to Free African Americans from North Carolina and Virginia" includes the Moore family as one of the families descended from freed slaves who had been indentured. For the full extracts of these court records and dockets, refer to Paul Heinegg's writings.[97]

Fannie Moore Cross, our Nana

"One Lord, one faith, one baptism" (Ephesians 4:5). Nana was the best grandmother in the world. When we were youngsters, my sisters and I would spend nights at her house while my mother and father were attending their social events or they just wanted to spend time together. From time to time, we would run down the street to Nana's house just to say hello or to deliver something from my mother or to pick something up or just to get a big hug and a kiss. In our teen years, my sister Barbara and I stayed with Nana when she became ill. She lived on Cooke Street at that point, and she was widowed. We would spend the night just in case she needed assistance or to be able to call family if an emergency occurred.

Prior to this, and before she became widowed, step-grandfather Charles Cross was often sitting on the porch at Eighteen Pearl Street. He had been stricken with Parkinson's disease and could not get around much in his later years. He was so wonderful and kind and Nana took such excellent care of him. He was dark and handsome with salt-and-pepper hair, and he was so very polished and always neatly dressed. All of Nana's sisters and brothers were stunning and very polished to me as well. They were very sure of and comfortable with themselves. They were properly raised and extremely blessed.

Church was one of our mandatory weekly outings with Nana. We were christened, baptized, and reared in the church. We were members of Grace Baptist Church in Waterbury, Connecticut, where Reverend Jonathan Reed officiated. Reverend Jonathan Reed is one of the recipients of the Silas Bronson Library Award for successful Waterburians, just like my sister, Barbara J. Hatcher, PhD. A beautiful elementary school has been named in his honor—an honor well deserved. He ran a strict church and insisted that all the children whose families were members of the church were educated to the best of their family's ability. My mother had played the piano at the church from time to time many years ago, particularly for Sunday school.

Uncle Oliver and Aunt Minnie Jones

My Uncle Oliver Jones and his wife, Aunt Minnie, the former Minnie Gatling, were like second parents to us, and they lived near us most of the time or at least a very short drive away. On the other hand, my mother's other brother, Uncle Joe, lived in a home a little distant from Waterbury. We would pack up a family picnic and my immediate family, to include my Uncle and Aunt Minnie, and sometimes other family members would travel to where he was located and we would have him with us for several hours on a special outing.

Uncle Joe so much loved music, and he was very excited when we were with him. He moved so gracefully and rhythmically to the sounds. I enjoyed watching him, and I would smile and clandestinely join in with the beat. Uncle Joe was cool. The time with Uncle Joe allowed me to practice my timing. I loved music, and I was a dancer. He must have been musically inclined like his brother Oliver who played the saxophone and my mother who played the piano. My Uncle Oliver and my father always ensured that he was well taken care of and that he was dressed very neatly and that he remained safe and healthy during our stay with him. He was unable to fully care for himself.

Aunt Minnie and Uncle Oliver had no children of their own, but they raised Aunt Minnie's sister's children as their own. These children, Lindora and Jimmy Gatling, were raised as my cousins, and though we are not blood, we were and are cousins anyway. Aunt Minnie, the former Minnie Gatling, was born in Waterbury. The Gatling family in Waterbury was and is very large. Lindora informed me that her immediate family consists of twenty persons to include her three daughters, her numerous grandchildren and now great-grandchildren. She is blessed and a very strong believer. I love her and her offspring dearly.

I must admit this side of my story is harder to tell because that unconditional love was indescribable as I recall the growing up aspect of my life. It is gratifying to remember the strong sense of love and family and difficult to know that they are no longer here. But I know each and every one of them is resting with the Lord. Yet it is so hard to put this unspeakable passion into words.

We didn't have to travel to another city to be with them. They were with us all the time since they often lived a block or two away. Even so, that did not diminish the love and warmth felt by those who lived elsewhere and who were not around us as much. It was just different.

My grandmother, Nana, had more than thirty siblings born to her father, Thomas Moore (twenty-three or more when you exclude those by the first wife who didn't live long). But these weren't the only children in this generation since her father's brothers had quite a few children as well. I was unable to locate any of her father's sisters in detail since I do not have their married surnames, but I do believe that some of these sisters and their families are automatically connecting to my tree on Ancestry.com. I may not have time to analyze this before the first print of this book, but I may do so in the near future.

But the number of children born to my great-grandparents Thomas and Adaline Moore numbered fourteen. I will focus mainly on them since I knew most of them personally and most were present in my life in my developmental years.

I estimate that with my grandmother's father's siblings, there were more than sixty and probably closer to seventy children born into that family in one generation. My mother would tell me that there were so many that she had not met most of them in her lifetime, and she still doesn't know most of their children or their children's children who may still be living.

As children, we would hear that our great-grandfather Thomas had children by two wives. He married my great-grandmother Adaline after his first wife, Flora Cardwell Moore, expired. On the Internet great-grandmother Adaline is identified as Adaline Rose. I believe Rose was her former surname and hot her middle name. The first wife had birthed sixteen children with eight or nine living before she passed. Childhood diseases were definitely present during those times, and they were deadly.

The second wife who was my great-grandmother Adaline had fourteen children. She was twenty years great-grandfather Thomas Moore's junior and together they continued to build this dynasty. Through this research, I am finally gathering the facts and learning who they are. I am told there could be other children birthed to other women.

As you can see, the Moore family has been present in North Carolina since about 1685 and just as the extract from Paul Heinegg's writing about the free Moore family is extremely long when compared to other African American families from the south, it speaks to the number of persons in the Moore bloodline. To connect so many persons to the family tree is historic yet interesting. It appears from Paul Heinegg's research that the Moore bloodline was free during the 1810 census, which was years before the Emancipation Proclamation.

Currently the Moore seed is scattered in different states and maybe in other countries. But they originally landed in North Carolina and travelled and relocated north on the East Coast. Other descendants may still live in North Carolina. During the earlier years, the vast majority of my ancestors lived somewhere on the East Coast but not farther south than North Carolina. I know some people with the last name Moore but I believe they may have been from a different Moore clan if their ancestors were not originally from North Carolina. On the other hand, there is a strong possibility that they are from the same clan and their seed started in North Carolina and we are related and don't even know it.

As for the Moore descendants, some still carry the Moore surname and others do not because of marriage. They may now live all over the United States and in various other places. Some do not carry the Moore surname though they continue to carry the Moore seed. Some of the married surnames that are beginning to connect to my family tree are Lowe, Lomax, Galloway, and Winchester. I already know about the surnames Jones, Cross, Stroud, Gilreath, Williams, McLean, Gatling, Anderson and Potts, to name a few. Again, when we were growing up, the family would simply say that there were at least thirty children in my grandmother's immediate family and many more in her generation since her father had several siblings. I was able to identify some, but I am almost sure that I have not identified all. My grandmother Fannie Moore Jones Cross, who we called Nana, was one of the children born to that generation. And yes, there were too many for us to even know and that is a fact.

As I complete this genealogy, I am overwhelmed, but not surprised, by the number of children produced by my great-grandfather Thomas Moore and his siblings. I would say a tribe or clan was created for the rest of our duration here on earth. More than sixty and closer to seventy children in one generation! That's a lot of children.

Let me introduce you to some of the Moore family. Farming was their occupation for many, many years. They owned farmland and most of the Moore males listed in the census were farmers. Other than farming and servitude, there wasn't much else to do. In fact, they had done it for so many years as free people according to court dockets back to 1683. For a long period of time, they were both taxable and "tithable," which indicated both property owners and free or freed people. As I stated earlier, those who were free and landowners sometimes married slaves or former slaves, and they produced children. What I learned in this research is that when Africans and other servants first arrived in the States, they were indentured. About seventy years later, the status for those who later entered or had not yet been freed was changed to slave. Those who were not free became a part of the transition from indentured servants to members of the African slave labor in America. The white man needed the African slave labor forever, and they wanted such labor to be free. Based on this, the intent was to now enslave them forever. But that was nonsense, and within time, that plan was defeated. The devil is defeated.

The Moore family appeared to escape this change in plan since they are often referred to in court documents as free servants, but not slaves. Anyway, the plan for slavery forever died within time and that is why we are here today. Thank you, Jesus.

Great-Grandfather Thomas Moore

This is what I know and what I have found during this study. My great-grandfather Thomas Moore (b. 1840) was born in North Carolina along with his other siblings. Great-grandfather Thomas was a farmer like his brother Alfred Moore who owned plenty of land. Alfred owned a lot of farmland in Cypress Creek, Franklin County, North Carolina. He had other brothers who I attempted to identify through census documents, and I hope that I am correct. It is so easy to pick up a wrong person along the way in your genealogical research. My advice is to just delete that person and anyone related to them and get back on track.

Prior to his marriage to great-grandmother Adaline, great-grandfather Thomas was married to his first wife, Flora. They had sixteen or more children with six or seven having died in their youth. Those whom I was able to track from the 1880 census and other census data are as follows: Nancy Moore (b. 1862), William Moore (b. 1867), Thomas Moore (b. 1868), Sina Moore (b. 1870), Rufus Moore (b. 1872), Lena Moore (b. 1874), Emma Moore (b. 1877) and Jesse Moore (b. 1879). After the 1880 census, they had three more children, twins, John Moore (b. 1880) and Mary Evelyn Moore (b. 1880) and the youngest child, Edith Moore (b. 1883). The census shows great-grandfather Thomas as mulatto and his wife, Flora, as black. In 1880, they lived in New Bethel, Rockingham, North Carolina, and his occupation was a farmer.

After the death of great-grandfather Thomas's first wife, Flora, he married my second great-grandmother Adaline (b. 1860). She was twenty years his junior. They had fourteen children, and they lived in Morehead, Guilford, North Carolina: Pinkney Moore (b. 1884), Hannah Moore (b. 1886), Lucy Moore (b. 1888), Fannie Moore (b. 1889) and William Moore (b. 1889), they were not twins and probably were born nine months or more apart, Lydia Moore (b. 1891), Daniel

Moore (b. 1892), James Moore (b. 1894), Oby Moore and Lizzie Moore who were twins (b. 1896), Adelle Moore (b. 1899), George and Annie Moore (b. 1900) who were twins and the youngest, Hubbard Moore (b. 1903). Living with them in 1910 are two grandchildren Ona Anderson (b. 1907) and William Anderson (b. 1909).

Great-grandfather Thomas owned the farm on which they lived. Tradition has it that the Moore family had plenty of farmland, and based on my mother's only visit there, the house owned by her aunt Lydia had living conditions much more up-to-date, and it far exceeded the living conditions of other African Americans such as those in rural Virginia and other parts of North Carolina. The way my grandmother and her sisters and brothers dressed and the manner in which they carried themselves when we were growing up was a good indicator that they came from good stock. They were well raised and committed workers and at least one was an "entrepreneur." Very proper and aristocratic they were, though very soft spoken but stern. This is what I remember about my great-aunts and great-uncles!

"For with God nothing shall be impossible" (Luke 1:37). In summary, great-grandfather Thomas had thirty or more children with six or seven of the children having died at a young age or during childbirth. He had a brother Alfred whom I am told had quite a bit of farmland and he himself had fourteen children. Census data definitely supports this. According to information obtained from the census, some of great-grandfather Thomas's children, to include my grandmother, would stay with his brother from time to time, and so would some other children maybe born to a sister or one of his children since their last name was different. Some of the brothers to include great-grandfather Thomas lived in close proximity to each other in Rockingham County and in close proximity to their dad, who appears to be Americus Moore. Thomas and Alfred definitely had more siblings, and I may have correctly identified a couple of them as listed below. There are probably more to be identified and recognized as family.

Located in adjacent land to great-grandfather Thomas are properties owned by at least two of his brothers, Squire Moore (b. 1848) who is listed as black and Stephen Moore (b. 1850) who is mistakenly listed as white by the US Marshall who was in charge of the census. They made assumptions on their own, and they based their assumptions on physical features and color of the skin. Remember Thomas Moore was listed as a mulatto in one of the census databases. So their hues could have been different, but the seed was the same. Also, David Cardwell and his wife, Eva, are living on Thomas's property, and he is listed as a laborer and is more than likely the brother to his first wife, Flora Cardwell Moore.

Great-grandfather Thomas's father had to have been Americus Moore (b. 1818). His farmland is located directly next to great-grandfather Thomas's farmland. Second great-grandfather Americus is married to Maria who is nineteen years his junior, so I am sure she is not the mother to great-grandfather Thomas and his brothers. Second great-grandfather Americus and Maria had three children: Ann Moore (b. 1865), Belle Moore (b. 1871) and Americus Moore (b. 1879). The mother to great-grandfather Thomas could have been Elizabeth. She was probably his father's first wife who birthed a child named Americus in or around 1839 or 1840 and had more children later. Again, this has yet to be confirmed and at this point is merely an assumption. But it was common for families to stay together and to live in close proximity to each other for survival purposes. So for now, I will list my second great-grandparents as Americus and Elizabeth Moore.

Members of the Moore family were farmers and owned plenty of land. As I continue to search, I believe I found another brother, Ivans Moore (b. 1848), who was possibly a twin to Squire, and he has a wife and five children. Without a doubt, there are more.

To capture all the Moore family will seriously require more research and a separate book. I was able to locate a couple of the brothers and their father because they are actually listed on the same census page and their farms are adjacent to each other. There could be other family members listed on the page before or after. Without the names, there is no way to go back or move forward on a page. Again, I would wager that there were more siblings especially since families produced more than two or three children even if it meant a second wife. My Moore ancestors definitely followed this huge child-producing pattern. I need more information and affirmations, so if you have some news for me, please come forward. God said to plant his seed and let it grow. Our Moore family did just that.

I do have some additional information regarding two of great-grandfather Thomas's children from his first marriage. Great-uncle and great-aunt, John and Mary Moore, were twins born to great-grandfather Thomas by his first wife, Flora. They were the youngest children along with another sister who was born after them. John was the father to our cousin Robert who lived in Waterbury, Connecticut, and was married to his second wife, Margaret Morris Moore, from Virginia. Information on the other children is scanty although more information keeps connecting to my tree on Ancestry. com as more people and census documents are uploaded.

We knew quite a bit about the Moore family from Robert when we were growing up. But most of the time this information became a little overwhelming especially since I was only a child. Several sets of twins were in the mix and we knew that twin births were in our genes. Robert was our earlier historian, and he often visited North Carolina and other places with his wife, Margaret, trying to put it all together. He wanted to know every person who was related to us. That was his mission.

Alma Sellers Moore was great-uncle John's first wife, and they had four children. The Sellers family supposedly owned a lot of property in Burlington, North Carolina. It is reported that John may have had four or five wives and children were produced from each of these marriages. Great-uncle John worked for R. J. Reynolds. On the R. J. Reynolds's plantation, John trained others on how to handle the thrashing machine used for cotton. He eventually moved to Harrisburg, Pennsylvania, and lived with his son Robert Moore and Robert's first wife, Cethia Moore, because of some surrounding circumstances that he had witnessed taking place on the plantation. I am told he had to leave for his own safety.

He must have gathered a little bit of income because I am told that he thought he was rich. In Harrisburg, he lived at least for a period of time in the same household with his son Robert (b. 1900) and three of his younger sons: Jeremiah Moore (b. 1903), John Leonard Moore (b. 1907) and William J. Moore (b. 1910). His wife, Alma, was not present. It is further reported that he had a child by a black Indian whom he had not married. The son Isaac mingled with the family and continued to do so in the later years. He was called Ike, for short.

Based on information shared with me by cousin Margaret, I know of three children still living and who came from this portion of the Moore seed, Mozelle born to cousin Robert, and Geraldine Adams and Carolyn Moore born to cousin Jerrey. I spent some time with Carolyn, her mother and her father Jerrey, when I attended Howard University. It is my understanding that Carolyn still lives in Washington DC and she has children.

Great-uncle John had a twin sister, great-aunt Mary Evelyn Moore (b. 1880), who married Chaffin Potts (b. 1878). According to census data, they had six children: Joseph Potts (b. 1896), Raymond Potts (b. 1905), Mary V. Potts (b. 1913), Willie Potts (b. 1914), Lester Potts (b. 1916) and Dorothea Potts (b. 1922). They lived in Portsmouth, Virginia, where their children were born.

I think I need a couple of volumes to cover the Moore side of my family. I was never able to know them all, and to the best of my knowledge, I have never met the children born to the first wife, or all their children, or their children's children, or some of the children of my grandmother's whole siblings and their children's children. Maybe it is time for a family reunion.

Again, third great-grandfather Thomas had a myriad of children. Some of the girls born to third great-grandfather Thomas and his first wife have not been located after the earlier census when they are living with their parents. If they married, it is impossible to find them without knowing the marriage surname. Again, many different last names are attaching to my family tree for those who are definitely Moore descendants. Also, there had to have been more sons and daughters born to second great-grandfather Americus Moore, who I am more than sure was my second great-grandfather. In fact, I am pretty certain of this.

Again, my mother used to say there were too many to ever know, and she wasn't going to try. She knew there were two wives and some twins involved. She knew all her aunts and uncles who were full sisters to her mother born to great-grandparents Thomas and Adaline with the exception of those who had died before she was born or by the time she would have been old enough to know them.

Great-Grandfather Thomas's Brothers

Great-grandfather Thomas had three brothers that I have located. I am almost sure there were more. His brother, great-granduncle Alfred Moore (b. 1849) married Lucy (b. 1846) and they had fourteen children prior to 1900 with eight children living. I was able to capture the names of thirteen of Alfred's children in all: Martha Moore (b. 1869), Mary Moore (b. 1872) Jerrie Moore (b. 1873), Lear Moore (b. 1874), Polly Moore (b. 1874), Narsissa Moore (b. 1876), Lillie and Lizer Moore who were twins (b. 1878), Louisanna Moore (b. 1879), Aggie Moore

(b. 1884), Jasper Moore (b. 1887), Winnie Moore (b. 1889) and John Moore (b. 1892). They lived in Cypress Creek, Franklin, North Carolina.

Great-granduncle Squire Moore has two nephews and a niece living with him on the farm, Nancy Moore (b. 1862), a nephew's name is slightly illegible and may be Bengal (b. 1873) and Samuel (b. 1879). Nancy Moore is a child of Thomas and the other two may have been as well.

In 1900, great-granduncle Squire is listed with his wife, Polly, and they begat children of their own. Data indicates they had seventeen children and seven lived. The children identified are: Robert Moore (b. 1887), Jonda Moore (b. 1891), Garfield Moore (b. 1894), Squire Moore Jr. (b. 1885), Mita C. Moore (b. 1887) and Charles Moore (b. 1900).

Great-granduncle Stephen is married to Ceila (b. 1843), and they begat three children, Harris (b. 1872), Stephen Jr. (b. 1874) and Frank (b. 1876).

Great-granduncle Ivans is more than likely another brother who may have been a twin to Squire. Ivans (b. 1848) married Rebecca S. Moore (b. 1858). They begat five children as follows: Jerrey L. Moore (b. 1867), James Moore (b. 1868), Mary A. Moore (b. 1874), Thomas H. Moore (b. 1878) and Adolphey Moore (b. 1880).

I know that the Moore children had children who had children and many of them I will never know. My cousin Robert Moore would bring anyone with the last name Moore to my mother's house in Waterbury and would state that this has to be a family member whether it was confirmed or not and especially if their family originated in North Carolina.

I can only discuss with confidence the members of the Moore family that I had direct contact with or who I heard conversations about or are otherwise confirmed as family members. They were blessed by God with so many children, and I am told that their farm in North Carolina was very large with nice quarters. I can believe this just based on how my grandmother, Nana, and her siblings carried themselves. Their dress was so immaculate and their clothes so perfectly ironed and pressed, and they stood straight in posture. At least one of the children enjoyed farm life and remained in North Carolina. I believe my grandmother was previously a laundress in North Carolina. "Is anything too hard for the Lord?" (Genesis 18:14).

NANA'S FULL SIBLINGS (parents: Thomas and Adaline Moore.) I am not sure if I captured everyone who was a full-blooded sibling to my grandmother, but I know from the census records that I have come very close. The children born to second great-grandparents Thomas and Adaline are listed below. I have captured what I was able to piece together and corrections may eventually be in order.

Great-uncle Pinkney Moore (b. 1884) moved to Columbus, Ohio, and had a lifelong marriage to Josephine Moore (b. 1896). According to census documents, they had nine children. Some of the grandchildren and great-grandchildren still live in Ohio and my cousin Margaret reminds me that the Moore descendants are scattered all over the United States and all over the world. Based on census data, the nine children I located on record are or were Cornelius (b. 1913), Thomas (b. 1915), Joseph (b. 1917), Alma C. (b. 1919), Naomi (b. 1919), Katherine (b. 1921), Nathaniel (b. 1922), Jennie (b. 1927) and Ruth N. (b. 1930).

Great-aunt Hannah Moore (b. 1886) was very well to do and owned several properties in Waterbury that she rented out. She lived in a very nice home off of Cooke Street and married Lyman Gatling. She was quite a businesswoman and very serious and stern. She graciously opened her home for our large family reunions. What I remember most was playing croquet on her large back lawn. I also remember her large front porch, which was screened in. She had no children of her own but raised her late sister Annie's children, cousins

Thomas and Louise Gilreath. Tom married Bessie, and they had three children born in Waterbury: Howard, Lionel, and Baron. Louise married William "Bill" Fogle and Diana is their daughter who now lives in Massachusetts.

Great-aunt Lucy (b. 1888) lived on Cooke Street, and all I can say is that all the sisters were so soft, yet stern and extremely well-dressed. She married William W. Mc Lean (b. 1887), and they had several children: Lareener (b. 1908), Iola (b. 1912), Mary E. (b. 1912), Leona (b. 1924), William (b. 1927) and Walter (b. 1930). I remember my cousin Leona and her husband, Buddy, who would have picnics and family gatherings at her home in West Haven. They had three children and Ronald is the only one I remember by name.

Grandmother Fannie Moore (b. 1888) was my Nana who I discussed earlier and who was married first to Joseph Allen Jones (b. 1888), my late grandfather, and then to Charles Cross after my grandfather Allen's death. My grandparents Joseph and Fannie had had five children altogether, but two died in childbirth or at a young age. Their surviving children were Oliver (b. 1908), Joseph Jr. (b. 1911) and my mother, Viola (private) and none by Mr. Cross. My mother dropped out of college at Virginia Union when her stepfather and her mother both became ill. They tried to keep their illness from her, but one of her classmates from Waterbury who was also attending Virginia Union advised her what he had heard about her family situation. Mom insisted on returning home to care for them. What a blessing. However, she did not have the opportunity to complete her education at Virginia Union.

Great-uncle William Moore (b. 1889) lived in Waterbury and married Aunt Grace. Aunt Grace had two children from a previous marriage, Buster and Virginia Lewis.

Great-aunt Lydia Moore (b. 1891) remained in North Carolina and never moved north. Aunt Lydia would come to Waterbury for family reunions. She married Will Williams, and they had a son, Robert Williams (b. 1921). Robert married Helen Williams, and they lived in Waterbury.

Great-uncle Samuel Moore (b. 1892) and great-uncle James Moore (b. 1894) must have passed before my mother was born or some years after. She is not familiar with them.

Great-uncle Oby Moore (b. 1896) was a twin to Lizzie, and he lived in Pennsylvania. It appears he and his wife did not have children.

Great-aunt Elizabeth "Lizzie" Moore (b. 1896) was a twin to Oby, and she lived in Waterbury and then in Stamford, Connecticut. Great-aunt Lizzie married Robert Stroud (b. 1892) and they had three children Edith Stroud (b. 1916), Robert Stroud (b. 1925) and James Stroud (b. 1928) who passed when he was young. Cousin Edith was very close to us, and she was born and raised in Waterbury. She married Ulysser Ralph, and they moved to Stamford. Their children are Doris, Carolyn, Alfred, and Marjorie.

Great-aunt Adelle Moore (b. 1899) must have also passed before my mother was born or some years after. She is not familiar with her.

Great-uncle George Moore (b. 1900) was a twin to Annie. He lived in Columbus, Ohio, and was married to Mary Moore (b. 1889). According to census data, their children were or are as follows: Lillie (private), Edith (private), Barbara (private), a new born in 1930, and Clara Moore Shivers (private) who still lives in Ohio. Clara and my mother are close, and they stay in close contact.

Great-aunt Annie Moore (b. 1900) was married to Cicero Gilreath, and she was a twin to George. Before her death, they had four children: Louise, Russell, Thomas, and Cicero Gilreath Jr. Again, great-aunt Hannah raised Louise and Tom after their parents died. Louise married Tom Fogle, and they had one child, Diana, who now lives with her husband and children in Massachusetts. Tom had three children, Howard, Lionel, and Baron. Howard lives in Waterbury,

Connecticut, with his wife, Josephine, and they have no children. However, there are a number of children born to Howard's brothers and probably to the next generation as well. I know of at least one set of twins.

Great-uncle Herbert (Hubbard) Moore (b. 1903) was the youngest and was referred to as "Hub" or Uncle Hub. My mother tells me that he was the character in the family. He lived in Waterbury and was tall and handsome. He had never married. My mother said in his earlier years, he would buy a new convertible it seemed like every year. He would come by his sister's house who was my Nana, and he would take my mother for a ride, and she loved it, convertible and all. She says when she was younger he was always styling and boy could he dress. She referred to him as Dapper Dan: sporty, tall, and debonair. He also had his personal moments that cousin Margaret and my sister Barbara so vividly recall.

The Jones Family

Mom's father was born and raised in Greensboro, North Carolina, but she had never met her grandparents or her aunts and uncles on her father's side. She was separated from her paternal family due to the early death of her father when she was only two years old. After moving to Connecticut, Mom only traveled south to see her mother's family in North Carolina once as a teenager and then to visit my sister who was attending the University of North Carolina at Chapel Hill. Grandfather Allen's immediate family wanted to meet Mom when she was just an infant, but they never had the opportunity to do so due to Mom's move to the north.

But a few of the family members from the Jones family had moved to Waterbury, her cousins Dorothy Miller Moore and Dorothy's parents, Haywood and Mabel Miller, and Haywood's sister Della Miller. These relatives at least helped to fill the missing link on the Jones side of the family. Dorothy Miller Moore was pretty close to my mother, her cousin, and they worshipped at the same church for years.

The Marriage of Grandparents Joseph Allen Jones and Fannie Moore

"My words are spirit and they are life" (John 6:63). My grandparents Joseph and Fannie Jones, both born around 1888, lived in Greensboro, Guilford County, North Carolina, when they married. They had four children with two still living at the time. The other two probably died in childbirth or shortly thereafter. Grandfather Joseph is listed as a lumber wagon driver. The two living children at the time were Oliver Jones (b. 1908) and Joseph Jones Jr. (b. 1911). Grandfather Joseph died around 1924 in Baltimore County, Maryland, and Nana died on December 4, 1962, in Waterbury, Connecticut.

Grandfather Joseph's mother was Mary Jones (b. 1849) and she had had eight children with five living. One of grandfather Joseph's brothers was Oscar Jones (b. 1884), a fireman. He was married to Julia (b. 1887), and he shows up in the census living in close proximity to his mother Mary and his brother Joseph. I have been unable to affirmatively identify the other children.

Dorothy Miller Moore

Several members of the Jones family moved to Connecticut. These are the only members of the Jones family that my mother knew well. She was close to her cousin Dorothy Miller Moore who was born in Greensboro, North Carolina. Dorothy moved to Waterbury with her father and mother, Hayward Miller (b. 1902) and Mable Ashe Miller (b. 1906), and they all lived in Wolcott, Connecticut, not far from Waterbury. There were other children born to this union: Lillian Miller (b. 1927) being one. Also, my mother's cousin Della Miller (b. 1912), sister to Haywood, lived in Waterbury or maybe Wolcott, and she was one of the first African American sales ladies to work in an upscale Waterbury clothing store, Worth's.

Cousin Della was always dressed so well, and she and her niece Dorothy were very attractive. She and cousin Haywood had another brother Clifford Miller (b. 1906). Their parents were Anderson Miller (b. 1876) and Mary Miller (b. 1884). The Miller family is the only connection to the Jones seed that is familiar to us.

In 1930, Haywood Miller and Mabel Ashe Miller are living with her parents, Alexander Ashe (b. 1876) and Ellen Ashe (b. 1878) in Morehead, Guilford, North Carolina, along with Mabel's brother, Haywood Ashe (b. 1912), and Alexander's mother, Emily Ashe (b. 1846).

Cousin Dorothy (b. 1924) died on March 9, 2012, after a long illness. She was a former schoolteacher and wife to Frank Moore who was also a schoolteacher in Waterbury. She had received her master's degree from Central Connecticut State University and was very active with the works of Mt. Olive AME Church where my mother and father were members. She had four children, one who is now deceased, and one grandchild.

There is not much more I can say about Grandfather Jones and his side of my family other than the fact that he was supposedly an awesome farmer and mason as well, and he probably owned farm land in Greensboro, Guilford County, North Carolina. My mother stated that according to her mother, there are markers where he owned land or built structures under his full name Joseph Allen Jones or by the name in which he was known, Allen Jones. She always remembered her mother referring to him as Allen.

My mother states that she does not remember her dad. He died when she was around two or three years old, and she never met her grandparents. It appears that her grandfather had already passed and her grandmother Mary Jones may have died shortly after my mother's birth. My mother Viola recalls that her mother told her that the rest of the Jones family constantly asked about her and wondered when they would have the opportunity to meet her.

Mom's brothers knew the Jones family quite well because for some years they lived with or adjacent to their paternal grandmother, Mary Jones, in Greensboro, North Carolina. One of my mother's brothers, Uncle Oliver, would travel south from time to time when we were children, but we never went with him. Records indicate that great-grandmother Mary was a widow and the earliest record I could find does not indicate her husband's name. So I do not know my great-grandfather's name or when he passed. According to my mother, other than those listed above, she never had the opportunity to meet the rest.

My Hometown and the Dubois Family Cheshire and Waterbury, CT

The Broken Dubois Link

It is definitely perplexing, though not unusual, that the family connection between W. E. B. Du Bois and his father's family was permanently broken. I used to ask why someone who had gained such notoriety and lived not far away from his kin folk where he was born in Massachusetts did not search for or contact his family in Connecticut, especially in his later years. He knew a little about his grandfather's second family when they moved to Massachusetts and even then it was scanty and disconnected. From his writings, he also knew that his grandfather Alexander, who was my third great-grandfather, had several children with my third great-grandmother Sarah Marsh Lewis, but he didn't appear to have ever met any of his aunts and uncles who would have been older than him, nor any of his cousins who would have been closer in age.

W. E. B. and the Dubois family appeared to have a permanent separation and the way in which his father left him and his mother must have bothered WEB. When these pains or denials are present, this type of separation is sometimes inevitable. So it is what it is. The pain from his father deserting him and his mother must have been excruciating. I still see these types of family separations occurring even today. It becomes rather emotional and only those who are subjected to this understand. This includes those who finally connect with parents and the family they never knew. I also find it ironic that he used Du Bois instead of the family name Dubois. An assumption can be made that he separated his name for a purpose, maybe indicating a permanent separation from the Dubois family. Again, this is merely an assumption.

My younger sister was named Viola Dubois Hatcher, a tradition of being assigned a female family member's original surname as a middle name to ensure that the surname and family history was not lost. My son, Watani Abdul Dubois Hatcher, carries Dubois as one of his middle names as well. My father had constantly stated that he believed the spelling given to my sister as a middle name may or may not have been the family's tradition. But he was right. Records indicate it was the proper spelling used by most of our ancestors. A few like WEB used other spellings though his progenitors did not spell it that way. Changing the last name from Dubois to Du Bois was something he decided to do for whatever reason. Nevertheless, you will find variations in the spellings for Dubois, the traditional spelling used by my ancestors. Other spellings include, but are not limited to, DuBois, Du Bois, du Bois, Duboise and even Dubose.

The Dubois Interaction throughout the Years

Cornelia Dubois Johnson Garner was the youngest child born to Francis Henry Johnson and great-grandaunt Mary Dubois Johnson, sister to great-grandmother Nettie. Cornelia's mother, great-grandaunt Mary Dubois Johnson (b. abt. 1868) married Francis H. Johnson (b. abt. 1865), and they had ten children. Two of the children, Rachel F. (b. 1892, d. 1893) and Francis Henry (b. 1894, d. 1895) died in their first year of birth and Ida Louisa (b. 1887, d. 1896) at the age of nine.

Great-grandaunt Mary Jane Dubois Johnson died on the 31 May 1941 in her home in Oakville. Listed in great-grandaunt Mary Jane's obituary are her living siblings at the time: Louise Ridley (a.k.a. Louise Sarah Ridley) and Nettie Dubois Hatcher. Based on my research and discussions with my cousin Asiila, the children born to Francis and great-grandaunt Mary were as follows: Alfred H. Johnson (b. abt. 1884), William E. Johnson (b. abt. 1885), Ida Johnson (b. 1896, d. 1887), Rachel Johnson (b. 1892), Frances Henry Johnson (b. 1894), Harold Plato Johnson (b. abt. 1897), Susie F. Johnson (b. abt. 1902), Elsie Frances Johnson (b. abt. 1903), Milton Raymond Johnson (b. abt. 1906) and Cornelia May Johnson (b. 1908).

Cornelia, the youngest child, and her husband, Leroy Garner, were extremely close to her first cousin one time removed, who was my father Theodore W. Hatcher Jr. and to my mother Viola. My sisters and I called them cousin Neil and cousin Roy. They meant so much in our lives, and they were always so supportive. When we were young children, most weeks we were either at their home in Oakville, Litchfield County, Connecticut, or they were at ours. The four of them had a standing Pinochle gathering on Friday, I believe, or it could have been on Saturday, and they alternated their gatherings in each other's home. I am sure these games were canceled from time to time since we spent a lot of time in Long Island, New York, on the weekends. They enjoyed each other so much. As young children, we would fall asleep on their couch. I can still hear the laughter. Cousin Neil had such a boisterous and heartfelt laugh. I also remember the gatherings and family picnics on their property, a rather sizeable piece of land. I have found a lot of pictures from the numerous gatherings with family members from all sides.

Cousin Neil and her husband, cousin Roy Garner, or Garner as she called him, were very special and two of my favorites in life and so were their children. Their children and my cousins were June, Leroy Jr. and Harold. Their children's marriages and their offspring are as follows: June and Arthur Rhinehart and their children with Joanna Rhinehart being the only girl and a seasoned actress/producer who lives in Manhattan, New York, and her brothers, Roy, Arthur Jr., Carl and Mark; I don't believe I left anyone out, and of course, I do not know the names of any of their children; Roy and Peggy Garner and their two children, Leslie and Leroy III (Chip), and then as time moved on Roy's second wife, Cher; and Harold "Deke" Garner, the youngest and his wife, Shirley, and their children Jackie (Asiila), Harold Jr., and Stephanie. Roy was an oncologist and Harold a lieutenant colonel in the military.

Harold recently informed me that he was the first African American to play basketball for the University of Connecticut. We are known for our firsts and you find out something new every day. Also, my sister earned her bachelor of art degree from University of Connecticut (UConn) and Harold's daughter Asiila advised me that she had attended UConn for a period of time as well. Again, Harold J. Garner is married to Shirley C. Garner, and he is a retired lieutenant colonel.

I miss cousin Neil as much as I miss my dad. They were a pair. When they both started aging, neither would move from their homes in Waterbury and Oakville, respectively, and my father defined her as "stubborn." What was ironic is that he was too. However, when challenged on this, his justification was that she was some years older than he was. He explained that their roots were buried too deep in

Connecticut and that neither one of them could ever move from there. To do so would be quite devastating. Besides, he could never leave his cousin Cornelia to fend for herself. He had to be there for her. Dad died on 23 November 2006, and cousin Neil died shortly thereafter on January 6, 2007, in a rest home in Southbury, New Haven, Connecticut.

Cousin Neil's granddaughter (cousin Asiila) and I became very close while both of us were living in Arizona and we shared many private moments together. She has two sons, Faheem Rasool and Muhammad Al-Muthakkir. Her husband is Ali. Her sister (my cousin Stephanie Garner) is married to Scott Koberstein, and they have three children, Garner, Ryan, and Malia. Her late brother (my cousin Harold or Hal as he was called) had four children with his wife, Iris Avila: Abigail Elizabeth, Jael, Josiah Bukki, and Hannah. I have just learned about Abigail's interest in our W. E. B. Du Bois roots. I hope this document provides her a wealth of information.

Our interaction with the Dubois side of the family would take a book. There was cousin Geraldine Lewis. She had two children Mary Jane and William who lived a couple of blocks down the street from us. Cousin Geraldine was one of the grandchildren of my great-granduncle John Dubois, who was one of the brothers to great-grandmother Nettie. We drove by cousin Geraldine's house for some of our travels away from the neighborhood. Whenever we passed by and if she was on her porch, my father and mother would say "wave to your cousin Geraldine." We would also see her on the porch sometimes when we walked to church.

Cousin Geraldine was very close to cousin Neil who in her earlier years would take a bus from Oakville into Waterbury in order to spend time with her cousin. She also spent quality time with my father, her cousin Ted. Cousin Mary Jane Cherry provided me a copy of her family tree, which was very useful in my Dubois search. She has two daughters and a number of grandchildren, and I believe another grandchild or a great-grandchild on the way.

I never heard much talk about great-grandmother's sister Sarah Louise or Louise Sarah Dubois and her family. However, Aunt Natalie had contact with them and was able to give me enough information about her and her children that allowed me to trace them for inclusion in this family tree. Sarah Louise Dubois (b. abt. 1866) was born in Cheshire, Connecticut. She married Leroy Ridley (b. abt. 1863) from Massachusetts, and they lived in Waterbury. One of their addresses in Waterbury was 297 Pearl Street. Living with them were a daughter Gertrude Allen (b. abt. 1882), their grandchildren Ruth Hale (b. abt. 1908), Alan Hale (b. abt. 1909) and Grace Hale (b. abt. 1911) who were Josephine's children with her husband, John Hale (b. abt. 1886). He was born in Waterbury, and Josephine was born abt. 1890 in Waterbury as well. Also, living with great-grandaunt Sarah and her husband, Leroy, are an unknown daughter's children, their grandchildren Gwendolyn Joseph (b. abt. 1915) and Alfred Joseph (b. abt. 1917). I always wondered after whom I was named and now I know. The Joseph children were born in New York and their father was from the West Indies. The mother to the Joseph children, great-grandaunt Sarah Louise's daughter, must have passed at the time this particular census was taken. Other descendents resulted from the marriage of the former Grace Allen, noted above, to Haile Allan Washington who like his wife was both born in Waterbury, Connecticut. They had two daughters, Brenda (b. 1930) and Edna (b. 1931) Washington who were born in New York where they lived.

Upon the death of great-grandaunt Sarah Louise's husband in 1925, records indicate that she moved with her grandchildren from Waterbury to Manhattan, New York, where her daughter Josephine had lived for years and had married Lawrence Richards who was born 1866 in New York. His father was born in New York as well and his mother was born in Virginia. Cousin Josephine and Lawrence were not together when her mother moved there and my cousin Josephine is listed as divorced.

Fourth Great-Grandfather Dr. James Dubois

One of our original ancestors was my fourth great-grandfather Dr. James Dubois, who was an ethnic French-American from Poughkeepsie, New York, who fathered several children with Bahamian slave mistresses.[98] One of his mixed-race sons was Alexander, my third great-grandfather who was husband to the former Sarah Marsh Lewis and both were parents to my second great-grandfather Henry A. Dubois. Poughkeepsie is located midway between New York City and Albany and is not far from the Connecticut state border.

Fourth great-grandfather Dr. James Dubois was born around 1750 or later and died shortly after 1810 when he was sixty or slightly older. Records indicate he had had a nonmarital liaison with one of his slave mistresses from the Bahamas, and they produced at least two children, Alexander and John. Fourth great-grandfather James Dubois died without a will and his property was taken by white relatives.[99]

I must state that researching this portion of our ancestry is less strenuous since our Dubois ancestors were also the ancestors of W. E. B. Du Bois. Data is readily available because of the notable W. E. B. Du Bois who was a pioneer sociologist and civil rights leader. WEB was my first cousin three times removed. In an excerpt from "the Autobiography of W. E. B. Du Bois: A Soliloquy on Viewing my Life from the Last Decade of Its First Century," (New York: International Publishers Co. Inc., 1968), pp. 61-77, WEB recounts his own ancestry back to sixth great-grandfather Chretain Dubois and his son Jacques who had a brother Louis. They were French Huguenots who migrated from Flanders to America. Perhaps a third son who spelled his name Du Bose went south. Louis and Jacques Dubois settled in Ulster County, New York. They were French-speaking immigrants.

From fifth great-grandfather Jacques descended fourth great-grandfather James Dubois, born about 1750, who became a physician in Poughkeepsie, New York, and migrated to the Bahamas and fathered my third great-grandfather Alexander in 1803 and his younger brother John.[100]

Dubois Ancestry Information Researched by Others

The information listed on the Internet equally applies to our family tree. I am not sure if it is in the public domain or if I as a descendant have the right to copy this information about our ancestors without first gaining permission. To be on the safe side, I will include the websites that you can access on your own. I find this information rather moving. It appears to be factual. This is the only side of my ancestry that I was able to trace past my fourth great-grandparents.

Surprisingly, via these websites, you will find other names to include ancient great-grandmothers from the Dubois side of the family and other ancestors as well. Taking our tree to the fifth and sixth great-grandparents is exploratory enough for me for this first round. But I may decide to conduct more research in the future. Also, in the mix are the names of some very famous people of French and white descent who are supposedly linked to our Dubois family. So don't be surprised if you find we are related to several notable Americans who are not African American whose surnames are Shriver, Weld, Patton, Lucas, and Brando. W. E. B. Du Bois is clearly documented to be a descendant of this bloodline and therefore related to these individuals.[101] You just never know. As you can imagine, I find it too heavy for me to absorb at this time.

If you are interested in researching this further, I refer you to the following websites:

1. Chretain Du Bois to W. E. B. Du Bois, posted 30 March 2007 7:35 PM GMT. 18 July 2012. <http://boards. ancestrylibrary.com>.
2. Chretian Du Bois, from Wikipedia, the free encyclopedia. 18 July 2012. <http://en.wikipedia.org/wiki/ Chretien_DuBois.>.
3. Dubois Family Association which includes W. E. B. Dubois in the heritage stated above at <http://www.dbfa.org/ membership.htm>.

The Dubois Family in Connecticut

"Remove not the ancient landmark, which thy fathers have set" (Proverbs 22:28). Last, but not least, I would like to introduce my Dubois ancestors who were born as full-blooded siblings as it relates to third great-grandparents Alexander Dubois and Sarah Marsh Lewis and to second great-grandparents Henry A. Dubois and Sarah Brown Dubois. Except for the very early descendants in France, New York, and the Bahamas, most of our descendants lived or were born in Connecticut. As is well-known, third great-grandfather Alexander Dubois was born in the Bahamas to a Bahamian mother. Though I have information on at least three generations further in this family connection, I will only cover those starting with Alexander Dubois in this particular section. Information about the earlier generations can be located on the websites I previously provided for the Dubois French heritage. Also, I recommend that you read the books and writings of W. E. B. Du Bois for particulars about his life and that of his father, second great-granduncle Alfred, who was a brother to my second great-grandfather Henry. They shared the same father.

The Dubois Family

Alexander Dubois (b. 1803 and d. 9 December 1887) was born in Long Cay, Bahamas, and married Sarah Marsh Lewis (b. 1804 and d. 9 July 1834.). She probably was born in New Haven, Connecticut. and they married on 4 May 1823 in New Haven. Alexander and Sarah were my third great-grandparents.

They had several children, among them is Henry A. Dubois born February 26, 1825, in New Haven, Connecticut. Second great-grandfather Henry married the former Sarah A. Brown (b. abt. 1827), my second great-grandmother, who was also born in New Haven. As discussed throughout this document, they had fifteen children.

A possible relative to Henry is Benjamin Dubois (b. abt. 1824) located in Connecticut, more than likely New Haven. Benjamin was a porter and married Ann Dubois (b. abt. 1820), who was born in Connecticut as well. They had a son Erastus, born abt. 1848 in New Haven.

Another relative is probably Diana Dubois (b. abt. 1828). She may have married, which makes it hard to trace her without a marriage license or surname. It was customary for a female to replace her surname with that of her husband in those days and it was not customary for the female to use the maiden name as her middle name once married, but she may have previously had a family name as a middle name.

John Dubois (b. abt. 1828) married Maria Dubois, and they had three children. John most likely was kin to Henry. His children's names were Washington (b. abt. 1858), Clara (b. abt. 1863), and Ida (b. abt. 1869).

There could have possibly been more relatives that I have not been able to identify. At one point I found a Reverend Alexander Dubois who was listed as black or mulatto, and he could have been a son or nephew or related in some other fashion. If I recall, he lived in New York.

Second great-grandfather Henry Dubois was born 26 February 1825 in New Haven, Connecticut, which is less than two years after his parents Alexander and Sarah Dubois were married on 4 May 1823. He appears to be the oldest child born to this union. Second great-grandfather Henry's full-blooded siblings, if any, will have to be further verified and more information may change these relationships.

Henry Dubois marries the former Sarah Brown (b. abt. 1827) around or about 1847. Henry Dubois is listed as a member of "Chesire's Black Community." His occupation in the 1870 census was listed as "laborer" and tax records show that he probably owned land and definitely had assets. They lived a good life, and he had a handsome salary for some years. They owned assets worth a healthy sum as well. They had fifteen children as listed below who were born in Cheshire, Connecticut. where they were raised.

My Great-Granduncles and Great Grandaunts and my Great Grandmother on the Dubois Side

Great-granduncle James H. Dubois (b. abt. 1847) and great-grandaunt Sarah Dubois (b. abt. 1848) were the eldest. Great-granduncle James, who was more than likely named after his great-grandfather, Dr. James Dubois, moved to Waterbury, Connecticut, for a while and lived in close proximity to some of his siblings. He eventually moved to Philadelphia, Pennsylvania.

Before moving to Waterbury and in 1870, great-granduncle James is located with his parents in Chesire where he is listed as a farmer with his brother Joseph listed as a farmer as well. He becomes employed as a janitor in Waterbury and then as a waiter at a hotel in Philadelphia. He marries the former Henrietta Hamilton, who was born in Virginia, and they have a son James H. Dubois Jr. (b. 1882). According to the 1910, census they had been married for thirty-one years. Their marriage would have taken place in about 1879. There were seven births that occurred with four living at the time of the 1910 census. I have located at least two of the other children: George Dubois (b. 1885, d. 1911) and Charles Dubois (b. 1887 and died as an infant in the same year.)

Sarah Dubois (b. abt. 1848) was next in line to great-granduncle James H. Dubois (b. abt. 1847). Again, they were the oldest children born to my third great-grandparents Henry and Sarah DuBois. After the 1850 census, I lose touch with third great-aunt Sarah who would have been twenty-two by the 1870 census. She probably had married and carried a different last name or she may have expired.

Joseph Dubois (b. abt. 1851) is listed as a farmer along with his brother James. I have no further information about Joseph after the census of 1870.

George Walter Dubois's death certificate is located in Chesire's vital records. He was born 18 June 1852 and died 22 June 1869 in Cheshire, New Haven, Connecticut, at the young age of seventeen.

Charlotte P. Dubois (b. April 1855) has a marriage record that is readily accessible in the Chesire Town Hall in Chesire, Connecticut. She married William Larkins from North Carolina on 26 December 1870. Their marriage was an after Christmas gift. She was sixteen, and he was twenty-two years old. They moved to Meriden, Connecticut. and they had several children who are listed below. Her husband, William (b. abt. 1848 in North Carolina), was an express driver in Meriden, which is in very close proximity to Waterbury and Cheshire.

Their children were Arthur Larkins (b. abt. 1871), Rosa Larkins (b. abt. 1873), Nellie Larkins (b. abt. 1875), Sadie Larkins (b. February 1877). Mary E. Larkins (b. December 1878), William H. Larkins (b. December 1880), and Lottie Larkins (b. August 1887). Also, living with them are twins Grace and Gladys Larkins (b. abt. 1906) who are listed as their grandchildren.

Louisa Dubois (b. abt. 1858) is only located in the 1870 census.

Eugene Dubois (b. abt. 1860) married Lettie (b. abt. 1860). She was from Bermuda, and they had one child, Alberta (b. abt. 1882). Their daughter was born in Bermuda as well. So at some point they were probably living in Bermuda. After a while they lived in Waterbury, Connecticut.

Jennie Dubois (b. abt. 1861) was another sibling. I have no information after the 1870 census. Like her sisters, it will be difficult to track her further without a married surname.

Thomas Dubois (b. 6 December 1862) married Susian (b. abt. 1865) from Bermuda, and they had one daughter, Nino, who was born in Bermuda as well. Like his brother Eugene, he may have lived in Bermuda at some point. After that, they lived in Waterbury, Connecticut.

John Dubois (b. 6 November 1865, d. 19 December 1923) moved to Pennsylvania where he married his wife, Mary Jane, who was born in Philadelphia, Pennsylvania. They eventually moved to Waterbury and had at least five children, some born in Philadelphia and others in Waterbury. Both John and his wife died in Waterbury.

My father was very close to great-granduncle John's granddaughter, Geraldine Lewis. Having been raised in Waterbury, my sisters and I were very much acquainted with cousin Geraldine and her children, Mary Jane and William. Cousin Geraldine Dubois Lewis just recently expired, and she was in her nineties, I believe. Third great-uncle John had at least four children: Geraldine's mother, Bertha Dubois Lewis, was one of them. My cousin Mary Jane Cherry (formerly Mary Jane Lewis), was named after her grandmother, Mary Jane Dubois.

Cousin Mary Jane Cherry and her family grew up down the street from us.

Mary Jane provided information to me about her family. Her second great-grandfather John Dubois was at the helm, which helped to unfold the mystery with W. E. B. Du Bois and the Dubois family. Her second great-grandfather John's death certificate confirms the Dubois children's parents as Henry A. Dubois and Sarah Brown Dubois. Mary Jane is as excited about this finding as I am since she had been working with my mother at my request to try to identify the relationships and our blood connection with W. E. B. Du Bois. We always knew there was a connection but we didn't know to what extent. Based on information provided by Mary Jane, the children born to great-granduncle John and Mary Jane Dubois are as follows: Laura (b. abt. 1890), Ida (b. abt. 1892), Sarah (b. abt. 1895), John Jr. (b. abt. 1897) and Bertha (b. abt. 1903).

Julia Dubois (b. abt. 1865) was another great-grandaunt. I have no information after the 1870 census. She may have married and therefore had a different surname or she may have expired.

Sarah Louise Dubois (b. abt. 1866) was another sibling who sometimes listed herself in future census data as Louise. She interchanged between Louise and Sarah. Some people during those days and even now were or are called by their middle names and from time to time they used or use both names. So her official name was either Sarah Louise Dubois or Louise Sarah Dubois. More information about her is found in other parts of this manuscript. I do believe her age is improperly calculated in the 1870 census along with the ages of her parents. I have therefore made an adjustment accordingly. She married Leroy Ridley (b. abt. 1863) from Massachusetts, and they had at least three children as follows: Gertrude Allen (b. abt. 1882), Josephine (b. abt. 1890), and an unknown daughter

(b. abt. 1895) who probably passed and whose children they raised.

Mary Jane Dubois (b. abt. 1868). Her name on Ancestry.com is translated as "Manee" in the 1870 census. Again, they probably had strong French and Bahamian accents or this was a childhood nickname. She married Francis Johnson (b. abt. 1865), and they had ten children as follows: Alfred H. Johnson (b. abt. 1884), William E. Johnson (b. abt. 1885), Ida Johnson (b. 1887), Rachel Johnson (b. 1892), Francis Henry Johnson Jr. (b. 1892), Harold Plato Johnson (b. abt. 1897), Susie F. Johnson (b. abt. 1902), Elsie Frances Johnson (b. abt. 1903), Milton Raymond Johnson (b. abt. 1906) and Cornelia May Johnson (b. 1908).

Charlie Dubois (b. abt. 1869) is next to the last child. I have no information after the 1870 census.

Last but not least is my great-grandmother Nettie Dubois (b. 23 September 1871). She and Henry A. Hatcher (b. 29 November 1870) married in 1893. They are already mentioned in detail in this document since they were our great-grandparents. Their surviving children were as follows: Theodore W. Hatcher (b. 23 May 1895) and Virginia O. Hatcher (b. 1903).

The 1860 and subsequent census databases show Josephine Dubois (b. abt. 1814) and Matilda Dubois (b. abt. 1816) listed as black and living in Waterbury. Could these have been two of Alexander's siblings who were also born in the Bahamas? It is hard to tell. But based on the rest of my research, they probably were related as were other African Americans found during this time in the states of New York, Connecticut, Massachusetts, and Pennsylvania. Most if not all who were African Americans with the surname Dubois were probably related, and they were part of the Dr. James A. Dubois seed that was planted in the Bahamas with one or more of his slave mistresses.

William Edward Burghardt Du Bois and his Immediate Family

W. E. B. Du Bois's life is well documented. Included are those who were descendants of our Dubois roots and some of their spouses and children. WEB's father was my second great-granduncle Alfred H. Dubois. Second great-granduncle Alfred (b. 1835) married WEB's mother, the former Mary F. S. Burghardt (b. 1833), on 5 February 1867 in Great Barrington, Berkshire, Massachusetts. They had one child W. E. B. Du Bois (b. 23 February 1868). Prior to his marriage, second great-granduncle Alfred served in the military with the US colored troops on the Union side. His rank was listed as private and then as undercook. He is listed on the African American Civil War Memorial (plaque number B-36).

Second great-granduncle Alfred lived in various places to include Milford, New Haven County, Connecticut, and Rutland, Vermont and in Agawam, Massachusetts. He and his wife, Mary Silvina Burghardt, divorced when WEB was young. She died in 1885 and second great-granduncle Alfred died in 1906. Both died in Massachusetts. WEB died many years later in 1963. According to his own writings, WEB never saw his father again after his father left his family when he was just a lad.

WEB was my first cousin three times removed. His first wife was the former Nina S. Gomer (b. 1877 and d. 1950). She was born in Quincy, Illinois. They married in 1896 and had two children born in Great Barrington, Massachusetts: Burghardt G. Du Bois (b. 1898, d. 1899) who died from typhoid fever and Nina Yolande Du Bois (b. 1900, d. 1961). The three are buried in Mahaiwe Cemetery in Great Barrington, Massachusetts. Nina Yolande had two marriages, first to Countee Porter Cullen, born 30 March 1903 in Louisville, Kentucky, and then to Arnett Frank Williams who was born 26 July 1910 in

Baltimore, Maryland. She and Arnett Frank Williams had at least one child who I believe to have been Yolande Du Bois Williams.

WEB's second wife was Shirley Graham whom he married in 1951. Shirley Graham Du Bois (November 11, 1896-March 27, 1977) was an American award-winning author, playwright, composer, and activist for African American and other causes. In her later years, she married the noted thinker, writer, and activist W. E. B. Du Bois. Along with him, she became a citizen of Ghana in 1961 after they emigrated there.[102]

She was born Lola Shirley Graham in Indianapolis, Indiana, in 1896, and was the only daughter among six children. She and W. E. B. Du Bois married in 1951, the second marriage for both. She was fifty-four years old; he was eighty-three. They later relocated to Ghana, where they received citizenship in 1961. He had been denied a renewal of his US passport because of his political activities. He died in 1963 in Ghana. In 1967, Shirley was forced to leave Ghana after a military-led coup d'état, and she moved to Cairo, Egypt, where she continued writing. Her surviving son, David Graham Du Bois, accompanied her and worked as a journalist. She died of breast cancer on March 27, 1977, in Beijing, China, where she had gone for treatment.[103]

There are other descendants whom I have not traced. For sure, WEB has a great-grandson, Arthur McFarlane, who is a Harlem native and a longtime employee of the Colorado Department of Public Health and Environment. Summarized above is a snapshot of my other Dubois ancestors and relatives that have remained unknown or unspoken about as family for so long. I hope to contact Arthur McFarlane to advise him of this portion of his family. I didn't get to know his great-grandfather, but I hope one day to meet Arthur. I do know my sister, Dr. Barbara J. Hatcher, has been in Arthur's presence at some of the numerous public health conventions. It does not appear that she ever approached him as family since we were still trying to verify the extent of our connection to WEB.

W. E. B. Laid to Rest in Ghana

Finally, when I visited Ghana in May of 2000, my tour included the former home of my first cousin three times removed, cousin W. E. B. Du Bois, and his personal mausoleum, which have now been turned into a museum. His wife, Shirley Graham, was cremated and her ashes are located just behind his granite coffin, which is above ground. I did not know before arriving in Ghana of this historical spot in Ghana and I had not remembered that WEB had died in Ghana until then. I was more than elated. I learned more about my first cousin than I had remembered. I learned about his connection to Chairman Mao Tse-tung who was the founder of the People's Republic of China and one of the founders of the Communist Party. He was also a poet. I learned of WEB's inability to return to the States because of his political connections and political beliefs.

I actually spent time in WEB's library, which was filled with books, awards, pictures of him and of his wife, Shirley Graham, and his honorary documents and hangings. There was a special case containing the academic gowns and hoods of WEB. Again, I could sense that this was family. I took pictures of this family encounter. At last, I had the honor to be in his presence, if only in spirit, and among his belongings. I advised the young guide employed at this historic site that W. E. B. Du Bois and my family were related by blood. He didn't respond but just glanced at me for a moment as if to be absorbing that thought as he stayed focused on his presentation.

WEB's home and its contents are well-preserved and the mausoleum appears to be cedar or some other well-preserved wood with red carpeting. It is important that the building is maintained at the required temperature for preservation purposes. The grounds too are well kept. However, I have recently been informed by a cousin on the Odrick side who visited there that the conditions are beginning to deteriorate. I will try to remember to follow up on this. On a plaque is written the following words: W. E. B. Du Bois: "One thing alone I charge you. As you live, believe in life. Always human beings will live and progress to greater, broader and fuller life. The only possible death is to lose belief in this truth simply because the great end comes slowly, because time is long."

The family of whom I was a guest hired a personal assistant to escort me during my stay in Ghana. Her nickname was Sistah Babe, and she was very educated, spoke quite a few languages and spent months at a time in England where she had business connections. She told me her business had to do with manufacturing and selling light bulbs.

Before heading to the home site of W. E. B. Du Bois, we passed one of the many circles, Danquah Circle, named after one of Kwame Nkrumah's cabinet members. Prior to that, we had visited the National Arts Museum and the memorial and statute of Kwame Nkrumah who was by the way the first president of Ghana who took his people's land back from the British. My father was acquainted with Kwame Nkrumah while at Lincoln University.

My father had another friend who lived in Ghana who established a job training and educational facility but his name escapes me at this time. While in Ghana, I also visited the Cape Coast castles where the slaves were held, and I learned quite a bit, and I experienced standing in "the Door of No Return." This was the exit used to board the Africans on the slave ships. In addition to this, one of the strangest experiences in Ghana, which totally caught me off guard was being regarded as just another foreigner by local Ghanaians and actually being referred to as "foreigner" or "white." I had been called a lot of names, but never "white." That was a first. I found out later that this was standard treatment of African Americans, and we were actually referred to as white based on our mixed heritage. The country's native term for whites in Ghana is "obruni." Nevertheless, visiting WEB's home and mausoleum was an honor for me. That is the closest to him that I had ever been. I continue to honor him as one of our ancestors who did so much to make our lives a blessing to others. Amen.

What an undertaking this has been! Please e-mail me at mmegjh@ aol.com with questions, corrections, or additional information. I welcome any edits as I consider a second edition of this book, *Souls*.

The Hatcher Descendants—My Immediate Family; Theodore And Viola Hatcher

Waterbury, Connecticut, other parts of Connecticut and places in New York and Massachusetts as well as Philadelphia, Pennsylvania, are where the majority of my earlier Northern ancestry settled. Others settled in Washington DC and other places on the eastern shore. I was born and raised in Waterbury, and I attended college in Washington DC where I remained for eighteen years. I didn't know at the time that a number of my ancient ancestors were from this area.

I give honor and respect to all my ancestors and relatives, known and unknown to me. In fact, I thank all those who were a major part of my growing up. I have mentioned a lot of my family in this document, but I mainly focused on the blood relatives for the purpose of determining our family's bloodline. I am so grateful to my parents who showered us with love and knowledge. I give them a special bow, and I give honor to our Father, which art in heaven. My parents and their families and the Father, the Son, and the Holy Ghost sacrificed so much to ensure success in our lives. Train up a child in the way he should go, and when he is old, he will not depart from it. Proverbs 22:6. The current descendants of all the ancestors listed in this book are my sisters, Barbara J. Hatcher and the late

Viola Dubois Hatcher, my son, Watani A. Dubois Hatcher and myself.

Current Descendants of All the Ancestors Listed in this Book.

Barbara Jones Hatcher

Barbara J. Hatcher is the oldest daughter born to Theodore and Viola Hatcher. She was born and raised in Waterbury, Connecticut. She is well educated and quite decorated with awards and recognitions for her accomplishments. She received her bachelor degree in nursing from the University of Connecticut, her master's degree in public health from the University of North Carolina at Chapel Hill, and her degree in philosophy (PhD) in nursing administration / health policy from George Mason University in Fairfax, Virginia, where she is now a professor in nursing. She is a descendant of the Hatcher, Dubois, and Odrick lineage and all other lineages mentioned to include the Moore and Jones seeds. Barbara J. Hatcher, PhD, MPH, RN, FAAN, is internationally recognized for her work as a senior public health policy maker. She has published and traveled extensively and was a member of the District of Columbia Army National Guard for fifteen years. She served as chief nurse of both the 115th Combat Support Hospital and the Mobile Army Surgical Hospital (MASH). She served in Saudi Arabia during Operation Desert Shield/Desert Storm. She was named a Fellow of the American Academy of Nursing and received the Trailblazer Award from the National Black Nurses' Association in recognition of her achievements. In 2009, she was inducted into the Silas Bronson Library's Waterbury Hall of Fame. Barbara has achieved many firsts as a nurse and as an

African American. She is founder of the Hatcher-Dubois-Odrick Group, a consultant company, and she is active in a number and variety of organizations in the Washington DC area. She is also a member of a number of state, national, and international organizations where she served in chief executive roles. She is a longtime member of the African American sorority Delta Sigma Theta Sorority, Inc., the largest African American women's organization in this country.

Gwendolyn Janice Hatcher

I am Gwendolyn Janice Hatcher, middle daughter to Theodore and Viola Hatcher. I was born and raised in Waterbury, Connecticut. For thirty-four years, I worked in professional government positions at various levels and for a few government agencies to include the District of Columbia Employment Services, US Office of Personnel Management, City of Tucson and Pima County. My most recent position was Human Resources director for Pima County, located in Tucson, Arizona, where I served for twenty-two years and held the Human Resources director position for sixteen years. I was one of the top-paid officials in local government ranks and the first African American to serve as Human Resources director for Pima County. Upon retirement, I was the ninth highest-paid official out of one hundred top city and county officials in the various cities, towns, and counties in Southern Arizona and the highest-paid African American female. I am now pleasantly retired. I served in various positions with local, state, and nonprofit boards and committees, and I was a governor's appointee to the State Personnel Board where I served as member and chair. The governor at the time was the Honorable Janet Napolitano who is now an appointee of our current president of the United States, the Honorable Barack Obama. I earned my bachelor of art degree from Howard University and my master of art degree in teaching from Trinity College, both in Washington DC. I received numerous awards and recognitions for my community activities and was recognized in the *Tucson Lifestyle Magazine* among "Women We Admire." I was a member and past president for a local leads group, "Women at the Top" and a former active member of the NAACP where I received national recognition as an "Unsung Heroine." I am an ordained minister and serve as copastor of Living Miracles Church of God, a church that my husband, Pastor C. C. McKesson, and I cofounded. I am mother to Watani and a member of Delta Sigma Theta Sorority, Inc.

Viola "Vicki" Dubois Hatcher

The late Viola "Vicki" DuBois Hatcher was the youngest child who died many years ago at a young age. She was just too young. She was born 22 May 1950 in Waterbury, Connecticut, and she expired on 19 August 1973, in Washington DC. She attended Central Connecticut State University in New Britain, Connecticut, and was very talented and skilled. Her favorite pastime was knitting, and she was quite the expert. We still have a couple of her products in our possession. She lived for a few years in Washington DC where she passed. We miss you little sis and know that you are in good hands as you rest with Dad and our Father who art in heaven.

Watani Abdul Dubois Hatcher

Watani Abdul Dubois Hatcher is currently the youngest descendant of the combination Hatcher-Odrick-Dubois-Brown-Jackson-Frisby-Brooks-Moore-Jone-Rose and others on our family tree. He graduated from Hampton University in Hampton Virginia. He holds a bachelor of science degree in marine and environmental science. He also attended the University of Arizona in Tucson, Arizona, and William and Mary College in Virginia where he took summer classes in radiation oncology and marine biology, respectively. He has worked in local government in Washington DC as special staff assistant for one of the DC councilwomen at the time. He currently works in the corporate world as an area sales manager for the high-end Bloomingdale's in the Home Department in the DC area. He has received numerous awards and promotions in the retail business and also enjoys working with community organizations and participating in sports. He is son to Gwendolyn J. Hatcher, nephew to Barbara J. Hatcher and grandson to the late Theodore W. Hatcher Jr. and grandson to Viola J. Hatcher. He is quite distinguished and a very fine young man who is also a Hatcher-Odrick-Dubois-Brown-Jackson-Frisby-Brooks-Moore-Jones-Brown-Riddle-Rose descendant. As I close, I thank God for the blood of Jesus. Alleluia and amen.

I HOPE YOU ENJOYED THIS JOURNEY IN SEARCH OF MY SOULS. I TRULY DID IN THE NAME OF JESUS.

ENDNOTES

1. Douglas Harper, "Slavery in Connecticut. Slavery in the North," 2003 <http://www.slavenorth.com/connecticut.htm>.

2. William Addams Reitwiesner, "Ancestry of W. E. B. Du Bois," page 6, 1 April 2007 <http://www.wargs.com/other/dubois.html>.

3. US Dept. of Commerce, United States Census Bureau, "Decennial Census. Historic Snapshot of the Nation." <factfinder2.census.gov/faces/nav/jsf/pages/wc_dec.xhtml>.

4. Douglas Miller. "My Soul Is Anchored in the Lord."

5. "Puritan Migration to New England (1620-1640)." <http://en.wikipedia.org/wiki/Puritan_migration...>.

6. <http://en.wikipedia.org/wiki/History_of_Connecticut>.

7. Douglas Harper.

8. Douglas Harper.

9. James Oliver Norton, "Weevils in the Wheat: Free Blacks and the Constitution, 1787-1860," George Washington University, 1985 <http:/www.apsanet.org/imgtest/freeblackconstitution.pdf>.

10. Alice Mick and Lula White, "Italians and Blacks in New Haven: The Establishment of Two Ethnic Communities," <http://www.yale.edu/ynhti/curriculum/units/1978/2/78.02.06.x.html>.

11. "Emerging from the Shadows, 1775-1819: The Black Governors." <http://www.hartford-hwp.com/HBHP/exhibit/03/1.html>.

12. New Haven, CT. <en.wikipedia.org/wiki/New_Haven,_Connecticut>.

13. Nat Turner. "NNDB Tracking the Entire World." <http://www.nndb.com/people/937/000110607/>.

14. Professor Quintard Taylor, "African American History Timeline:1701-1800, University of Washington." <http://www.blackpast.org/?q+timelines/african-american-history-timeline-1700-1800>.

15. Dred Scott v. Sanford. <en.wikipedia.org/wiki/Dred_Scott_v._Sanford>.

16. Douglas Harper.

17. "Goffe Street Special School for Colored Children." <en.wikipedia.org/wiki/Goffe_Street> and Jean Sutherland, "Examining the African American Role in New Haven History: Pride in the Past, Hope for the Future." Yale New Haven Teacher's Institute. <www.yale.edu/ynhti/curriculum/units/1993>.

18. Mick and White.

19. Mick and White.

20. Inflation Calculator. <http://www.westegg.com/inflation/infl.cgi>.

21. George M. Guignino, "The Farmington Canal 1822-1847: An Attempt at Internal Improvement." <http://www.yale.edu/ynthi/curriculum/units/1981/cthistory/81.ch.04.x.html>.

22. "The Barite Mines of Cheshire." <http://www.cheshirehistory.org/barite_mines.htm>.

23. Pioneers/Yale African American Affinity Group, YAAA, Yale University. <http://www.yale.edu/yaaa/pioneers.html>. 7/20/2012.

24. Mick and White

25. Mick and White

26. Dixwell Avenue Congregational website, UCC website. <http://www.dixwellchurch.org/our_history.php>.

27. Dixwell Avenue.

28. Dixwell Avenue.

29. American Treasures of the Library of Congress. <http://www.loc.gov/exhibits/treasures/tri108.html>.

30. "Black Opera: An Interview with Opera Singer: Taimo Kujichagulia-Seitu." <http://sfbayview.com/2009/black-opera-an-interview-with-opera-singer-taiwo-kujichagulia-seitu/>.

31. American Treasures of the Library of Congress.

32. American Treasures of the Library of Congress.

33. Suzy, "Identity Crisis, Sweet Daddy Grace," 1/27/2006 <http://suzy-identitycrisis.blogsport.com/2006/07/sweet-daddy-grace.html>.

34. Wikipedia, the free encyclopedia, "United House of Prayer for All People." <http://en.wikipedia.org/wiki/United_House_of_Prayer_for_All_People.>.

35. Mick and White

36. Mick and White

37. Mick and White

38. "Race and Appearance of Jesus." <en.wikipedia.org/wiki/Race_and_appearance_of_Jesus>.

39. "W. E. B. Dubois." <http://students.cis.uab.edu//eshay07/page2.html>.

40. Randall K. Burkett, Emory University, "The Reverend Harry Croswell and Black Episcopalians in New Haven 1820-1860", 2003. The Northern Star: A Journal of African American Religious History, Volume 7, Number 1 (Fall 2003)

41. William E. B. Dubois, Darkwater, Voices from within the Veil (New York: Harcourt, Brace and Howe, 1920) p.8

42. Wikipedia, "Agawam, Massachusetts." <en.wikipedia.org/wiki/Agawam,...Massachusetts>.

43. Burkett 8.

44. Burkett 8.

45. Burkett 8.

46. Doctors Without Borders, "Haiti: MSF Increase Hospital Capacity in Earthquake-Affected Areas," January 9, 2012 <http://www.doctorswithoutborders.org/news/article.cfm?id=5721&cat=field-news>.

47. Haiti.

48. "New Haven, Connecticut." <http:/en.wikipedia.org/wiki/New_Haven_Connecticut>.

49. "Shinnecock Indian Nation." <http://en.wikipedia.org/wiki/shinnecock_Indian-Nation>.

50. Steve Sailer's iSteve Blog. Shinnecock "Indians" Get Their Casino. <http://steve.blogspot.com/2009/12/Shinnecock-Indians-get-their-casino.html>.

51. "Hempstead, Long Island, N.Y. History." <http://dunhamwilcox.net/ny/hempstead_hist.htm.>.

52. Anne Hartell, "Slavery on Long Island." 1943. Nassau County Historical Journal, 16 August 2012, <http:/longislandgenealogy.com/slav/htm>.

53. Anne Hartell.

54. Taken from Szucs, Loretto Dennis, "Research in Census Records." In The Source: A Guidebook of American Genealogy, ed. Loretto Dennis Szucs and Sandra Hargreaves Luebking (Salt Lake City: Ancestry, 1997). William Dollarhide, The Census Book: A Genealogist's Guide to Federal Census Facts, Schedules and Indexes, Heritage Quest: Bountiful, Utah, 2000. Source Information: Ancestry.com. 1850 United States Federal Census [database online]. Provo, Utah: MyFamily.com, Inc., 2004. Original data: United States. 1850 United States Federal Census. M432, 1009 rolls. National Archives and Records Administration, Washington DC.

55. Christopher Verga. "Slavery in Suffolk County."

56. Verga 2.

57. "Congress Abolishes the African Slave Trade." <http://www.history.com/this-day-in-history/congress-abolishes-the-african-slave-trade.>

58. The Slave Mutiny on the slaver ship Meermin. <http://www.pbs.org/wnet/secrets/featured/slave-ship-mutiny-about-this-episode/674/>.

59. "Exploring Amistad at Mystic Seaport." <http://amistad.mysticseaport.org/timeline/atlantic.slave.trade.html/>. Also, "Slave Ship." <http://en.wikipedia.org/wiki/Slave_ship>.

60. National Park Service, "Amistad Story." <http://www.nps.gov/nr/travel/amistad/amistadstory.htm>.

61. Research Guide to African American Genealogical Resources at the Connecticut State Library. <http://www.cslib.org/blagen.htm, pg 4>.

62. Hartell.

63. Hempstead, L. I., New York 1850 Federal Census. <http://www.rootsweb.ancestry.com/~nynassau/1850hnhc.html>.

64. Mick and White.

65. Ushistory.org, "A Brief History of Philadelphia, Philadelphia

66. History." <http://www.ushistory.org/philadelphia/philadelphia.html.>.

67. Ushistory.org.

68. "Slavery in the North, Emancipation in Pennsylvania." <http://www.slavenorth.com/paemancip.htm>.

69. "Slavery in the North, Pennsylvania."

70. "Slavery in the North, Pennsylvania."

71. "Slavery in the North, Pennsylvania."

72. Patrick J. O'Hara, "The Philadelphia Bible Riots." <http://www.aoh61.com/history/bible/phila_bible_riots.htm.>.

73. O'Hara.

74. Ushistory.org.

75. Slavery in the North, "Race Relations in Pennsylvania." <http://www.slavenorth.com/pennrace.htm>.

76. Slavery in the North Race.

77. Slavery in the North, "Slavery in Delaware." <http://www.slavenorth.com/delaware.htm.>.

78. Underground Railroad, Routes and Landmarks, <http://www.whisperofangels.com/routes.html.>.

79. Slavery in Maryland, Smithsonian Anacostia Community Museum.

80. Slavery in Maryland.

81. Virginia African Americans, <https://familysearch.org/learn/wiki/en/Virginia_African_Americans>.

82. Virginia African Americans.

83. Carole L. Herrick, Image of America McLean. 2011 Arcadia Publishing, Charleston, South Carolina.

84. Powhatan Indian Tribe History. <http://www.accessgenealogy.com/native/tribes/powhatan/powhatanhist.htm>.

85. Powhatan. <https://en.wikipedia.org/wiki/Powhatan>.

86. Paul Heinegg, Free African Americans of North Carolina, South Carolina and Virginia, Introduction. <http://www.freeafricanamericans.com/introduction.htm>. 25.

87. Daniel C. Littlefield, Carolina Professor of History, University of South Carolina, *The Variety of Slaves.* <http://nationalhumanitiescenter.org/tserve/freedom/1609-1865/essays/slavelabor.htm>.

88. *Littlefield.*

89. The "Secret" of Interracial Sex. <http://www.shmoop.com/colonial-virgina/law.html.>.Thunderbird Archeological Associates Incorporated, Phase II, Archeological Investigation, page 31.

90. "Remembering McLean's African American History," The McLean Ear. 3 May 2010, <www.themcleanear.wordpress.com/2010/05/03/457>.

91. "Waterbury, Connecticut" 18 July 2012. <http://en.wikipedia.org/wiki/Waterbury,_Connecticut>.9/6/2012.

92. 20th Century Waterbury, Waterbury Time Machine. <http://search.aol.com/aol/search?query=20th+Century+Waterbury it=keyword_rollover>. Also, Timexpo in Waterbury, Connecticut Presents the History of the Wristwatch. <http://voices.yahoo.com/timexpo-waterbury-connecticut-presents-history-8110308.html?cat=8>.

93. The Rambler, Transcription Sunday Star, 9 June 1918.

94. Dayna Durbin Gleaves, "Slavery across North Carolina." <http://www.learnnc.org/lp/pages/1919?style+print>.

95. Heinegg 1.

96. Heinegg 1.

97. Heinegg 1, forward Ira. <http://wwwfreeafricanamerican.com/Moore_Murrow.htm>.

98. "The Person. My Birth and Family." <http://media.pfeiffer.edu/lridener/dss/DuBois/DUBOISP1.HTML>.

99. "W. E. B. Du Bois," 26 September 2007, <http://en.wikipedia.org/wiki/W._E._B._Du_Bois>.

100. Reitwiesner.

101. Chretain Du Bois to W. E. B. Du Bois, posted 30 Mar 2007. 18 July 2012, <http://boards.ancestrylibrary.com>.

102. "Shirley Graham," from Wikipedia, 6 Feb. 2013, <http://en.wikipedia.org/wiki/Shirley_Graham_Du_Bois>.

103. Graham, Wikipedia